THE POWER OF EXPLOITATION

Barry Z. Masser

Parker Publishing Company, Inc.

West Nyack, New York

Library of Congress Cataloging in Publication Data

Masser, Barry Z
The power of exploitation.

Includes index.
1. Influence (Psychology) 2. Success.
I. Title.
BF774.M37 158,.1 79-12022
ISBN 0-13-687160-7

Printed in the United States of America

The Power of Exploitation

Also by the author:

$36,000 A year In Your Own Home Merchandising Business, 1978, Parker Publishing Co., Inc.

What the Astonishing Power of Exploitation Will Do for You

This is a brutally frank book about a potent subject. Exploitation is very likely the most powerful force one human being can bring to bear on another. Its impact can take on immense proportions. Constructively applied, it has the capacity to build empires; irresponsibly used, it can be awesomely destructive.

Because exploitation is that powerful, it is commonly used by the most respected individuals, institutions and corporations in the world. In fact, it is so tightly woven into the fabric of our lives that *there is simply no way we can escape the impact it has on our day-to-day activities and careers.*

But, ironically, it is never discussed by its users—or described in books. Until now, it has been a kind of secret weapon carefully guarded by the influential. *These remarkable pages provide the truth about exploitation as it has never been told before!*

This book comes directly to grips with the stark and sometimes harsh realities about using people. For example, it gives you a rather shocking look at the fact that manipulation is effective because most people are weak—they actually *resign themselves* to becoming victims of those who practice the use of exploiting others for their own purposes.

You may find parts of this book personally disturbing. But these pages are *not* intended to bring you joy through meaningless platitudes about "how to succeed." They *are* intended, through clear step-by-step explanations of exploitive tactics at work, to give you the muscle you'll need to control people and events.

Every chapter is a self-contained program that can quickly and automatically change you from a follower to a formidable wielder of influence over others. This remarkable information will give you the dynamic but *practical techniques* you need to rapidly become an adept handler of people . . . a force to be reckoned with.

Look at these examples:

- You'll see how a maintenance worker used *fear* on his boss as a means of gaining executive status in a company that had taken him for granted over a period of years. You'll find out how *you can do the same thing in your life.*
- You'll see how a beginning real estate agent is building the biggest, most prosperous operation in his city through a brilliantly executed strategy of *promises.* It's perfectly honest, and *you can do it as easily as he does.*
- You'll see how a woman, average in every respect, uses the force of *flattery* to get big raises and promotions. She advances faster than better qualified competitors in the company. *The following pages show how you can do exactly what she does.*
- You'll see how an ordinary employee dramatically enhances his life by demanding far more than he ever expects to get. It's simply part of *building illusions of power. You can put these hard-hitting tactics to use at once.*
- You'll see how a salesman turned things around in his life by adopting the immensely potent "attack defense." *You can begin using it today,* and you'll see a startling difference in the course of your existence within days!
- Have you ever used *silence* as a weapon? A department store buyer uses it with devastating effectiveness. Do you know what to do with your *eyes* to get control? Do you know how to *listen* in order to command others? The chapter on building an *authority/success image* includes stories of how eminently successful people use these

manipulative tactics to get their way *and how you can use them to get YOUR way.*

- In the chapter on *downgrading,* you'll see how a public relations man uses the "set-up/knock down" game to keep an iron grip on his employees and clients. If you supervise people—or ever hope to—*you have to know how it works!*

- Powerful people understand how to *build power structures* that keep them in positions of supremacy in both their business and social environments. This chapter brings you the step-by-step ways to do it. For example: An auto parts clerk achieves the position of general manager *by knowing how to utilize common rumors to his advantage.*

- You'll see how a young woman actually stumbled upon the remarkable strength of *assertiveness,* then developed a way to use it to attain tremendous forcefulness in every aspect of her business and personal life. *Her formula is yours for the taking.*

- Finally (but every bit as important as preceding information) you'll see *how to become manipulation proof.* In one case, an executive finds that saying "no" gives him new respect and weight in his dealings. In another, a woman learns to see through a bluff, and reaches unprecedented control of her life as a result. This chapter supplies protection against every manipulative strategy *that might be used against you.*

This book contains *scores* of examples like the ones sampled above. Each is highly detailed, and vividly illustrates the steps you have to take *to come out on top.* Each tactic is clear-cut, logical and *effective.* You *don't* need special skills or training to make them work for you. You can be yourself, and begin controlling people and events *today!*

Barry Z. Masser

Table of Contents

The Power of Exploitation

1

How the Towering Force of Exploitation is Used to Command the Direction of Every Human Activity

If You Don't Exploit . . . You'll Be Exploited

You have a clear-cut decision to make: If you are one of the people who allows others to control your life, you can continue along that path and try to derive every available benefit you can possibly squeeze from that situation. However, if you want to *break* the pattern of control that has governed your life, you must immediately set about the task of mastering exploitation strategies. You must hone your manipulative talents to the point where merely *talking* to another person will enable you to evaluate the extent to which that individual can be used.

You must understand *and believe* that there is *no neutral ground.* A purely defensive posture will invariably fail to protect you from being used. There are no spectators on the stage of life—only actors and directors—the dummies and their manipulators. Arbitrary resistance to manipulative requests will only result in your exclusion from events, and you can't win anything that way.

If you expect to enter a new job, a love affair, a contract, or even a bridge club, and have it function on a totally equitable give-and-take basis with no demands, concessions or advantages to either party, you are seriously deluding yourself. As a passive bystander, either life will pass you by, or you will be exploited each and every time, beyond a shadow of a doubt.

Therefore, you must face the reality that every social or business contact you make will include the unasked question of *who will eventually become the dominant influence and who will be dominated.* If the relationship flourishes and continues, the answer will become known in time. As surely as the sun rises, one entity will be used for the purposes of the other at some point in the future.

To avoid domination by others, you *must* become an exploiter in your own right. You *must* take positions of command in every relationship you enter. When you do so, you'll find that most people slip quickly and easily under your control without the use of force.

To command will seem as natural to you as breathing. This is true by virtue of the fact that most people *want* to be led. They offer absolutely no resistance to domination; they welcome being told what to do. When leaderless, they tend to flounder and drift with the tides.

The Amazing Phenomenon of Why People Allow Themselves to Be Used

One of the most fascinating truths you are likely to encounter in reading this book is the one we just touched upon; people, in practically every instance, seem to welcome being used by others. They don't simply cave in to exploitation—or concede victory to their adversaries after a bitter struggle for control—they actually appear to express *relief* at being controlled.

Perhaps psychologists can provide clinical answers about why this phenomenon occurs. But for our purposes, let it suffice to say that the basic underlying cause is *human conditioning* combined with the illusion that *to be used is perfectly normal.*

The conditioning that takes place in almost everyone's life starts early. From childhood, we are subjected to an endless stream of reasoning from our parents, business leaders and teachers. The words they say may vary, but the message is always substantially the same; "If you do as your superiors say, *you* will someday be handed the reins of power and leadership. On that magic day, it will be *your* turn to harvest the benefits."

In our naiveté it all seems perfectly logical. "Someday" means that we have not matured enough for positions of responsibility. We are told that our educations have not advanced sufficiently for us to be entrusted with money or power and our experience is not extensive enough to qualify us for the better things in life. In addition to that apparently flawless wisdom from our mentors, we learn that it is necessary and proper to wait in line. We simply must not try to rush the process of advancement. We don't dare take what we want until the way has been cleared by the powers over us. To make the waiting more palatable, we are given token raises and other symbolic rewards for our slavish adherence to the rules of the establishment.

Thus, from our earliest years, we are lulled into the outrageous belief that we will achieve success by heeding the simple-minded advice of the very people who have already *been* exploited—or by those who now want to use *us!*

These are the myths that have been perpetuated by the exploiters over the years. They were conceived and subsequently popularized precisely in order to keep us childishly hopeful that our labors will be rewarded "someday." Our parents and teachers have swallowed it, and heaven knows, most of our fellow workers have become believers. All of them are willing and convincing actors in this bizarre fiction we witness as we grow up. Most of us conform to it because we know no other way, and we proceed to fall neatly into the hands of the exploiters.

Every Moment of Your Daily Life Is Affected by the Forces of Exploitation

The lifetime of programming that prepares us to accept the short end of the stick would seem to be enough of a handicap to overcome in handling exploitation, but there is more; *we enter a world that has been meticulously rigged to suck us in.*

Astute people would probably be able to avert manipulation *if* they could clearly perceive the traps that are strewn in their paths. But the pitfalls are so adroitly hidden—and blend in so well with the scenery around us—that steering clear of coming under someone's influence is extremely difficult. Each exploitive strategy we are exposed to is carefully designed to strike directly at our points of vulnerability. Every one of them is intended to

an economist who had at his command a gold mine of fascinating data about trends in business, investment strategies, tax shelters, and so forth. Jack discovered that this man possessed a storehouse of information but had no idea whatsoever on how to market it. He had contacted Jack with the hope that some of his financial expertise would fetch a small fee if included as an article in the newsletter.

Jack saw that his current customers—stamp collectors all over the country—would continue to buy the newsletter as long as it brought them facts in that field. But, if the size of the publication could be *doubled,* with the added pages of valuable pointers from a qualified economist, the potential market would be far bigger.

Jack offered the man a nominal flat fee for a certain number of articles each month. The economist couldn't have been more delighted, as he could make extra money simply by writing down information that was already in his head. While his name would not appear in the newsletter, it was of no great concern, for it was really only the fee that mattered to him.

As Jack's growing newsletter gained popularity, scores of other opportunities were placed before him on the proverbial silver platter. One of the more important ones was exclusive sales distribution for a series of booklets on money management. Jack figured that the readers who were responding to the economist's articles would also buy the booklets at three or four dollars per copy. He was right—he sold them nearly as fast as they were printed.

Today, some ten years after his modest beginning, Jack K. has many thousands of subscribers who not only read his newsletter, but buy a fortune in pamphlets, books and stamps offered in its pages. *He is considered a foremost authority in fields he knows very little about,* because he has skillfully developed sources of information who are *eager* to practically *give away* valuable facts and figures!

This fascinating case graphically illustrates the fine line that can separate taking advantage of people and *using them constructively.* It's a classic example of sound exploitive strategy. While Jack K. does, indeed, profit handsomely from information he gets from others, *he gives his sources reasonable compensation* in wages that they probably would not have received anywhere else.

Exploitation Is Not Evil or Unethical

So exploitation can and should be beneficial for both the user and the used. It is a means by which average people can vastly improve their standard of living and their ability to deal with life as it really is. As this chapter has stressed, there are few *practical* methods aside from exploitation that ordinary people can utilize in order to substantially enhance their lives and break the control others have over them. As this book emphatically demonstrates, most of us begin life hopelessly locked into certain levels of accomplishment and prosperity. There is virtually no hope of escaping to higher planes unless we learn to use our fellows as a ladder that we can use to climb out of the muck. There can be no harm in doing this, since most of the people we'll manipulate seem bound and determined to remain at their assigned levels in life.

While almost nothing can be gained by preying on the less fortunate, there is certainly nothing immoral about getting other normal people to help you attain your goals as long as they also profit in the process.

What it finally comes down to is this: Exploitation cannot be considered unethical because it builds opportunities for people to whom such chances rarely come. While it is true that the individuals used are busily making lives for the exploiters better, it is also true that they are adequately rewarded for their efforts. The system makes use of these people, but it generally provides enough compensation to keep them satisfied.

Why Exploitation Commands Personal and Business Respect

What of the attitudes of people who are used? Do they look at the ones who command with bitterness and envy? No. One of the perverse aspects of a free enterprise society is that power commands respect. It usually makes no difference to people how your strength was attained. If you are victorious, you have earned undying esteem with no questions asked.

A case in point is the famous owner of a professional athletic team. Although an acknowledged tyrant, he has become a national idol because his squad won the division championship. His methods are never questioned by the great majority of people who admire his accomplishments. Even the occasional adverse publicity he receives in newspapers and magazine articles seems to be drowned out by the accolades he gets from the general public.

The harsh truth is that unless you win, you will gain the respect and admiration of practically nobody except your immediate family. The exploited class rationalizes this by saying, "But at least I can sleep nights," as if one's conscience is somehow tied to the amount of influence he or she commands. Besides, by all indications, most of the powerful sleep as well as the powerless, but their beds are in places like the Riviera, the Bahamas and other exotic corners of the world.

Again, this book does *not* advocate taking advantage of people, but it does recognize the fact that personal strength is the one human attribute that is universally looked up to by almost everybody. If you are not accustomed to handling the thunderbolts of power, it is perfectly normal for you to view that kind of awesome strength with apprehension. You are apt to feel that the possession of control over people and events will make you conspicuous—an object of contempt to the people you manipulate. The truth of the matter is that the ability to exploit will bring you unprecedented popularity and respect. Based on the above stated principles of human nature, it can be no other way.

The mastery of control over people and events produces another mystique that works in favor of the exploiter. When you use people, it automatically begins to attract others who feel you can "do something" for them. There is no greater feeling of exhilaration than when you are approached by an individual who wants to contribute his or her energies and talents to your cause. It begins to happen almost as soon as you have started using these tactics, and it builds with astonishing speed. Before you realize what has happened, you very often have more people putting themselves at your service than you could use in a lifetime.

Thus, any misgivings you may have about the ramifications that newly acquired power may have on your professional reputation, your family standing or your position in the community are unfounded. Becoming a user of people through legitimate means will dramatically enhance every facet of your life. You will find yourself more highly esteemed than ever before.

The Story of Donald M's Kingdom of Influence

Proof that ethically handled exploitation can command personal and business respect is demonstrated in the following story.

Not too long ago, Donald M. was one of countless starving songwriters trying to break into an industry that was overcrowded with established names. On more than one occasion, he had to ask friends and relatives to loan him enough money to keep the electricity turned on in his tiny apartment.

The first milestone in his remarkable career came within just one year of the day Donald turned from stockbroker to flat broke composer. One of his first songs was recorded by a popular group. This moderate success was followed by genuine stardom. He proceeded to produce a composition that was recorded by one of the top female vocalists, and it won immediate acclaim—and earned Donald a gold record for selling over a million copies. This major accomplishment got him a lucrative contract with a large studio. Then, one of his melodies was selected by the studio as the score for a motion picture. This song also went quickly to the top of the popularity charts and earned him a second gold record.

Despite his rise to fame and prosperity, Donald never forgot the manipulating that had taken place in his dealings with agents, studios and established stars. In fact, almost every person in a position of power used the desperation of hopeful outsiders to get what they wanted. More often than not, the starving beginner would eagerly sign away a brilliant piece of music or lyrics just for that "first break."

Seeing this process at work from his present vantage point—from the position of power he *now* occupied—Donald immediately saw how incredibly effective it could be. He would now be able to use his new prestige to obtain top music from aspiring unknowns at the lowest imaginable rates and at terms totally favorable to *him*.

Donald spread the word that he was looking for up-and-coming talent, and the procession to his studio started at once. His name, by now magic in the entertainment industry, held the promise of recognition to beginning composers. So they came to Donald and presented their best work. In the huge volume of scores he received, there were several gems. Donald easily obtained the rights to these for the mere pledge of a little possible income in the future—and mention of the writer's name on a record label.

Donald had made the swing from composer to producer. He had first propelled himself into a position of influence in his industry, then had *used* this influence to gain power over the many thousands of people who regularly strive for success along the same path he himself had recently traveled.

Although it became common knowlege that Donald consistently offered very, very little for highly promising music, he nevertheless commanded the respect and admiration of everyone who came to him for an audition. *The fact that he was obviously using his prestige to further his own interests did not seem to matter in the least to the men and women he exploited!*

How this Power Can Work for You

Of this, there is little doubt: Most people are convinced that all exploitation originates from the men and women who occupy positions of power—or by those who control great wealth. But the fact is that *you can use others for personal gain no matter who you are—regardless of what your financial standing happens to be.*

Example: Through manipulative tactics, an $8,000 per year furniture salesman established a center of power in the store he works in. From this base of influence he managed to attract an *additional $8,500* in commissions and, soon afterwards, attained the store managership. This man *certainly* did not begin with power. He was, in fact, near the bottom of the heap when he started this job. The exploitive strategy used in this instance was *flattery*. The salesman artfully complimented both customers and fellow employees to gain his objectives. These methods are covered in detail later in this book.

Example: A housewife dramatically transformed her life from an existence of daily drudgery to one of sparkling excitement. Through manipulation, she took total command of community leadership, and now basks in the enormous popularity that comes with it. Her highly effective campaign of manipulation was based on the building of a *power structure* using a mix of exploitive methods. She would first flatter in order to gain initial control, then threaten by innuendo to get her way and, finally, set clique against clique to further strengthen her leadership. This woman became undisputed chief in her social environment *strictly by virtue of her astute appraisal of people,* a skill defined for you in the following pages.

Example: An office machine service representative, normally destined to a boring career at mediocre wages, ended up as national service manager for his large company. He did it through an exploitive strategy of *fear* that just about *anyone* can use. This individual had nothing when he started except for the desire to come out on top—and enough savvy about using others to reach the top quickly. His tactics were based on telling customers that the machines they owned were on the verge of breakdown. He would build relatively minor malfunctions into serious problems in the minds of office managers, thus clearing the way for trade-ins on new machines. The consistently high sales to customers he personally serviced came to the attention of his superiors and led to rapid promotions (of course *he* led the way in pointing out the profits to higher-ups!) More about fear in a later chapter.

Again, you do *not* need renown, connections or wealth to make the currents of influence flow *to* you *instead of from* you, as they probably have been doing so far in your life. You do *not* need special talents or natural gifts to effectively use exploitation for personal advancement. True, an individual fortunate enough to have a certain inborn genius may find the path to power somewhat more clearly defined than a person without such genius, but the prizes brought by absolute control are no more difficult for that ordinary citizen to seize when exploitation is practiced.

We're All Part of a Puppet Show—Why Shouldn't YOU Pull the Strings!

Having dispelled the widely held notion that the word "exploitation" represents such unholy acts as those practiced by *Oliver Twist*'s Fagan and his band of child thieves, we come to the primary points of this book: Prestige, power and wealth will invariably go to those who succeed in utilizing other people for various legitimate purposes, and such new strength can do nothing but elevate the business and social standing of its holder.

Having read this far, you should also be convinced beyond any question that your environment has been stacked to work in someone else's favor. True, you may have been granted a comfy niche in this infernal machine where you are able to go about your business and produce a satisfactory living. But you should have no more illusions about where the major benefits ultimately go. A career of labor will accrue to the benefit of your employer.

Hopefully, you can also recognize signs of the conditioning you have been exposed to since the first days of your learning. Perhaps you can see that it is *not* normal for you to jump at the commands of the people around you, and you can now begin to combat the unreasonable desire you have always had to please your superiors. If so, you are at the threshold of making the most important transformation of your life.

The transition from led to leader can be compared to the mindless puppet which is suddenly able to cast off the strings, leave the stage and promptly take control of the dummy that, moments before, had danced at his side. This dramatic change in roles does *not* depend on one's willpower or ability to change personalities. Money or influence has absolutely no connection with an individual's capacity to assume personal command of people and events. It is done solely on the basis of *applying specific strategies in circumstances where they are known to be effective.*

Therefore, if you have even the most basic understanding of people, you should be able to select and use the exploitive tactics that fit a particular situation. It will work more often than you would have dreamed possible.

In terms of the immediate and future direction of your life, there are probably no pages in print anywhere on earth that hold the explosive seeds of change that the ones in this book contain.

2

Unleashing the Thunderbolts of Influence and Authority Locked Inside You

Before we get into the specific step-by-step methods of manipulation, it is vital that we take a close look at who you think you are . . . and who you *could* be if you wished to make some easy-to-accomplish far-reaching changes in your life.

We briefly discussed programming in the first chapter. Before you can strongly control others, *you must break the pattern of programming that has taken place in your life, and you must shatter the belief structures that have been built inside you by well-meaning relatives and friends since you were a toddler.*

Right now you are undoubtedly rigged to *respond.* This chapter will show you how to change all that. It will describe how you can become absolutely immune to exploitive commands from others. Then, when you are rid of those shackles once and for all, you can use the same techniques to become a *giver* rather than a receiver of commands, a ruler of strength and authority instead of a follower to be used at someone else's whim.

We will now explore the incredible power of your mind and how you can use it to make almost any changes you please. The human brain is thought by many to be the ultimate computer. A scientist recently said that if a *miniaturized* computer could be built to match the power of the human mind, it would fill the entire Empire State building in New York! *That's* the kind of potential we're talking about!

There may be as many as 5,000 different ways to harness the power of the mind, and all of them are more or less effective. They range from self-hypnosis to Yoga. This chapter discusses only one of many methods. The reader is urged to use this or one of the other techniques to develop enormous new powers of the mind. Almost any public library will have information about the various systems of mind control. These powers will more quickly bring you the skills taught by this book, and will make the practice of leadership easier.

How Self-Conception Can Determine How Far and How Fast You Go in Life

The image you have of yourself can go a long, long way toward determining what you accomplish in life. If you see yourself as physically beautiful—and *really believe it*—you will begin to feel more attractive, and start to appear that way to others. It has been proven time and time again. If you see yourself as financially successful, it's usually just a matter of time before money begins to flow in your direction. There are thousands of well-to-do people in the world willing to swear it's true.

Why is self-conception such a strong force in shaping your life? For some of the following reasons:

1. Self-esteem is one of the first assets you will gain when you change some of the conceptions you have of yourself. Self-esteem is important, because you must genuinely *like yourself* before anyone else will like you. And when people like you, success and power become far easier to obtain.
2. When you *think* certain things about yourself, you tend to eventually *become* those things over a period of time.
3. If you have bad feelings about yourself, it's often the result of criticism from people who don't understand who you are or what you want—and couldn't care less (this is the faulty programming mentioned before). A different self-conception will make criticism from others much easier to deal with.
4. When you are able to *be yourself* in every aspect of your life, you'll be much more comfortable—and far more effective at everything you attempt, because you won't waste any more time, energy or emotions apologizing to those who want you to do things *their* way (usually to benefit them).

Remember, we're talking about *your susceptibility to manipulation* now. In other words, your self-image can either make you a pushover . . . or the one who does the pushing. In this chapter, you are going to discover an amazing way to become who and what you want. You will learn how to *eliminate the vulnerabilities that might be making you an easy target for exploiters.*

The way these astonishing personal changes can be made is through *visualization*. Thousands of physicians and scientists are now exploring the interrelationships of mind, medicine and physical/mental health. They know that something unexplained happens when patients are encouraged to use the power of their minds to control the workings of their bodies. There are many names for this extraordinary new science: Integral Medicine, Patient Resources, Total Mind Power, Imagery, Psychic Healing and scores of others. Each name means substantially the same thing. Any human being who follows certain steps can utilize enormous mind power which, under normal circumstances, lies absolutely dormant. This vast dynamo of sleeping energy can prevent and cure illness and bring about dramatic changes that would have seemed utterly impossible only a decade ago.

You will now see precisely how this colossal power can be harnessed to your everlasting advantage.

Using the Mysterious Unused 90 Percent of Your Mind in Controlling Yourself and Others

Most physicians and scientists agree that the average person goes through life and never comes close to utilizing even 10 percent of the brain power he or she was endowed with at birth. *Visualization* is one very good way to tap that vast unused reservoir of power.

As we just mentioned, an increasing number of doctors are teaching their patients how to reach into this rich vein of strength in order to help combat ailments that do not respond to, or are beyond the control of, conventional drugs and therapy. The principle here is that *the mind,* through visualization, often *gains the ability to influence certain workings of the body.* It is reported that the technique is effective in a startling number of cases. Therefore, it appears certain that you can make yourself a far more forceful person by using visualization, even if you are now as average as apple pie.

Not even the most prominent specialists understand why visualization works. Despite astonishing advances in virtually all fields of medical research, the human brain remains one of mankind's deepest mysteries. The only basics that are understood about reaching into the dormant power of the brain through visualization are these:

1. *Concentration is not necessary, but relaxation is.* When you create a visualization for the purpose of dealing with an area you want to improve (the steps in doing this are covered shortly), the first few minutes must be spent in *relaxing*. When you relax, the mind tends to focus into a fine laser. Then, it turns inward to your *subconscious* where the new power lies, where the reprogramming will be accomplished.

2. You must *believe* that you have the *capacity to change!* You are not a "product of your environment", "too old to change" or any nonsense like that. View yourself as a wall that has received a dozen coats of paint over the years. Consider each coat a veneer of belief that has been imposed on you by *someone else*. The real you is not the last coat—the one that's visible. You can strip away the old paint—the old programming—through the power of your mind and discover the person you *really* are!

3. You can use visualization to *change* virtually *any facet* of your personality. Therefore, you can strengthen yourself in precisely the areas where you feel weak. Whether you find yourself overly susceptible to exploitation by others and/or reluctant to seize the reins of power, you can now *do* something about it in no uncertain terms.

Five Simple Ways to Quadruple the Power of Your Mind

Whatever you do, don't let the words "power of your mind" frighten you. Thousands of people would eagerly testify that the feat of changing faulty programming does not require intelligence, concentration, willpower or special training. The secret to this accomplishment is in daydreaming—in *visualizing* yourself as the person you *want* to be and *repeating* the daydream at least twice a week over a period of time until the changes start to take shape.

The process of visualization, when correctly done, serves to train the brain to command the body. The steps given to you are basic rules for creating your own visualizations that can make big, big changes in your life, starting immediately.

The basic procedure in putting together a visualization is to construct an imaginary event in which you perform some act in exactly the way you would like to perform it. The imagined event should be five to ten minutes in length from start to finish. It can be about *anything* in your life. For example, if you want to improve your golf game, you would create a visualization of yourself stepping up to the ball and hitting it a long distance with a perfect swing. You would see the ball (in your mind's eye) soaring through the sky directly at the flag on the distant green.

In this particular instance, it would be necessary for you to understand the basic anatomy of that "perfect" golf swing so you could imagine it accurately and so your body would learn the correct timing and movements.

If this pleasant daydream was repeated often enough, it would gradually begin to take strokes off your game; your muscles would start to obey the new commands from that reprogrammed corner of your mind.

Or, let's say you have always had a fear of people in positions of authority. This has put you under their control, because you have had difficulty standing up to these individuals. The cure might be a visualization in which you imagine yourself dealing with several especially powerful people in a meeting, perhaps negotiating on a high level. You see yourself getting the advantage—withstanding their most ruthless arguments and threats. In this meeting, you always have sharp answers and ask penetrating questions that ruffle the composure of the big shots seated around the conference table. You are finally the decisive victor and achieve absolute dominance over your formidable adversaries.

That's the general idea. Now, let's discuss the specific step-by-step method for creating these almost magical visualizations:

1. The visualization can either be written out by you, or recorded on tape in your voice. Either way, it must be in your own words and in just the way *you* see things happening. Remember, your mind will respond most readily to programming *you* provide. Don't worry about making your visualization a masterpiece of literature. Its primary purpose is to describe you doing a particular thing flawlessly.

2. Before the beginning of the visualization itself, you should include a minute or two with directions to yourself to *relax*. As mentioned before, this tends to focus the mind and direct it to the subconscious where reprogramming will occur. Ideally, the sessions you have should be free from outside distractions, and you should be mentally and physically at ease. That's why the best time to have sessions is just before retiring for the evening. Directions to relax and focus the mind may sound something like this:

   I feel no tensions, no anxieties of any kind. Every muscle in my body is relaxed. I am totally comfortable. My mind is untroubled by everyday cares and is free to soar, free to clearly see the things I will soon ask it to see . . .

   When you manage to relax yourself in this way before starting the visualization, your mind will do a much better job of clearly seeing the pictures you have created. Remember, concentration *is not necessary* . . . but a state of calm *is* important.

During this focusing stage, it can help to see yourself in a setting that is especially pleasant to you. You could be swaying gently in a hammock, reclining in a field of soft grass in the middle of an open field, snuggled up in a sleeping bag under the stars, or anything *you* personally like. Whatever setting you select, be sure to describe as much about the sensations you would feel as possible.

3. The visualization must include a number of instances where you perform *as you would like to perform.* As soon as you have completed the relaxation and focusing phase, you begin your visualization. Let's go back to the example in which you are to negotiate with four corporate presidents:

   I enter a conference room and take the chair at the head of the long table. I am here to negotiate labor contracts with the presidents of the four major automobile manufacturers. They are waiting for me to begin. The tension in the room is explosive, but I am totally relaxed and absolutely confident.

   The corporate president on my left glares at me and says, "My company will never agree to the outrageous terms you want." I look straight into his eyes and reply, "You'll agree and sign this agreement within ten minutes when I tell you what I should be asking. You'll be grateful to me for making my first offer as reasonable as it is."

   You see yourself bluffing, threatening, flattering, humoring and convincing the high-powered executives in the room to get your way. You *feel* the influence start to flow to you—and you *use it to win.* You get a strong feeling that there is nothing those people can do or say that can keep you from getting whatever you want. They become mere clay in your hands.

4. The story you invent must call for the use of all five of your senses: Smell, touch, sight, hearing and taste. This use of each sensory mechanism in your brain seems to strongly reenforce the new programming you are install-

ing. It also serves to make your visualization much more vivid and real.

Evoking the senses is rather easy, and fun. Here are several examples of how you can do it:

The sense of smell can be introduced by having one of the auto company executives light up a two dollar cigar. You can imagine smelling the wafts of blue smoke as they swirl about the conference table.

Touch can be imagined by feeling yourself tapping a pencil on the table as you impatiently wait for one of your adversaries to make his point. Or, you can *feel* elation as you destroy his argument with one of your clever rebuttals.

Sight would be satisfied in this case by describing each individual around the table in detail and by observing exactly how the room looks. You can include the color of hair, shape of face, expression of the individual as you move toward victory and so forth.

The hearing sense can be stimulated by giving each person a certain kind of voice; gruff, smooth, menacing, apologetic or frustrated. You'd hear laughter, doors slam, the far-off sounds of traffic from the street below and scores of other sounds.

Taste can be visualized when you are served coffee or tea during the crucial meeting or as your mouth goes dry during an especially difficult part of the talks.

No matter what the nature of your visualization—and regardless of what subject it is intended to deal with—each sense can be used to bring it to life in your mind.

5. *Repetition* is an important key to making visualization work as well as it should. The fantasy you develop must be repeated until you begin to see results. Two sessions per week is a good start. This might continue for a month or two, then drop off to once a week. After awhile, you'll notice that you no longer have to *read* your visualization or listen to it on tape. It will become totally familiar to you in every detail—stamped indelibly on your mind. That's

when the programming begins to take hold and change your old ways of doing things.

After a sufficient number of repetitions (the number varies depending upon the individual), the scene you visualized *becomes part of you.* Read about how a man changed his life by putting the power of his mind to use on a problem.

The Way Allen B. Manipulates Large Crowds Through Visualization

One of the most effective one-on-one salesmen in his company, Allen B. simply could not address large groups of people. The ability to do so would have easily doubled his income since an important part of his responsibilities was to give presentations to assemblies of potential customers at conventions and trade shows.

Despite well-prepared speeches and thorough knowledge of his material, Allen went to pieces before the gaze of hundreds or even dozens of people. His reactions were feelings of nausea and sometimes severe vertigo. The notes would swim before his eyes, and he would stumble, stammer and invariably make a mess of his talk.

Allen was astute enough—and had sufficient insight—to realize why this terrifying personal problem haunted him as an adult. As a child, his speech retained unfortunate traces of baby talk when he attempted to pronounce certain words. The other children in his school classes openly laughed at him when he was called upon by the teacher. Yet, his associations with other individuals were never marked by this ridicule. Thus, Allen's strong aversion to speaking showed itself only when he found himself in group situations.

All the will power Allen could muster failed to overcome this deep flaw in his personality, and concentration failed just as miserably. He went through this agony until he was in his mid-thirties. It was then that Allen read about how self-image could bring about both mental and physical changes. Since nothing else he had tried through the years had worked to correct his problem, Allen figured he had absolutely nothing to lose by attempting it.

The salesman learned that the key to changing his faulty programming was visualization. He had to *see,* in the privacy of his own imagination, things happening *the way he wanted them to happen.* He was to actually daydream about himself speaking powerfully and eloquently to a vast throng of attentive people. He was to create this fantasy exactly the way *he* imagined it—*not* the way a doctor or other stranger envisioned it: it was, after all, *Allen's* mind that was in need of reprogramming, not an outsider's. Therefore, the new programming *had to come from Allen himself.*

Following the recommended procedure, Allen sat down and wrote out his visualization: He described himself stepping up to the podium before the crowd and delivering a stirring address about his products. In order to completely remove any possible threat from the audience—and to make everyone out there as vulnerable as he felt—*Allen chose to see every member of the audience naked.* There was no chance he could be ridiculed by anyone in that condition!

Two or three times each week, Allen held sessions with himself. He would first relax deeply, then begin thinking about every detail of his carefully constructed fantasy. In effect, he was *reprogramming his mind* to eliminate his obsessive fear of public speaking.

It worked, and as the months passed, Allen became stronger and more self-assured during his talks. He continued his private fantasy sessions—and he also continued to see his audiences sitting before him without a stitch of clothing. In time, he gained supreme control over his listeners at trade shows. Needless to say, his income and importance gained as rapidly as his stage presence.

The Secret of Becoming the Person You Really Want To Be . . . Starting Today

Now that you have at your fingertips the potent force of visualization to make sweeping changes in yourself, how will you put it to use? How will you achieve, *today,* the first tangible signs of enormous new power?

It's one thing to have the *way* to get where you want to be, but another thing to be able to zero-in on exactly where the changes should be made. The next pages of this chapter will give you simple but highly effective methods for evaluating yourself—for finding out *where* visualization should be used to bring about the changes you desire.

The really amazing thing about these methods is that you can begin using them *today!* You are now aware that the practice of visualization takes no experience, learning or concentration. The same thing is true of pinpointing your areas of need; you can begin *immediately* the process of looking at yourself critically, which is the first step in decreasing your susceptibility to manipulation and increasing your influence over people and events.

Using the Perfection Transfer Technique to Develop Your Personal Power

Imagine the person you could be if you had the capacity to select the best qualities of all the strongest people you knew and could plug these qualities into your own brain. The Perfection Transfer technique gives you that extraordinary ability!

This amazing system of improvement consists of two basic steps:

1. You choose a person who has strong attributes in an area where you feel deficient, then you study the characteristics which make that individual effective and *write them down in fine detail.*

2. You create a visualization, incorporating everything you know about your "perfection model." In this fantasy, *you* become the person being studied, and *you* gradually begin to take on those strong characteristics you have admired.

There is no longer any reason to envy the personality strengths you see in someone else, no longer reason to ask, "Why can't I be what he is?" Now, within a reasonable length of time, you can *take for yourself* virtually any strengths you desire! Most people practically consume themselves wishing they were somebody else but never do the first thing about improving themselves. They are the losers—the ones almost always used by those who make the effort to make themselves stronger. The Perfection Transfer technique is, then, a way to *escape* the exploited class and a way to become a user of people in your own right.

The particular quality you choose to transfer to yourself from another person should be one that will *directly enhance your personal influence.* Obviously, it would not be of any great value for you to admire, say, the juggling ability of an associate. But it *would* be a distinct benefit to study the way a vice president skillfully supervises employees. Other possible areas to study are:

1. The power of persuasion.
2. The ability to command attention.
3. The way a person dominates fellow employees.
4. A quality of firmness apparent in those who lead.
5. The knack of gaining the respect of supervisors.

The particular trait you select in your perfection model must be one that is *outstanding.* It should be the one thing that the person does with distinctive skill—and far more effectively than anyone else you've ever seen before. The more outstanding it is, the easier it will be for you to *identify* the things the person says and does to make it work as well as it does. This, of course, will make creation of your visualization relatively easy.

When selecting your first perfection model, take care to choose a person close enough to conveniently observe. The more often you see the individual, the better you will learn to understand all the little things about his behavior that can be transferred to you through visualization. Being near your model is also advantageous in terms of comparing; when you are able to check your progress against the person you are using, you can measure your personal development much more accurately.

Rita G's Three-Stage Formula for Turning Painful Weaknesses Into Commanding Personality Forces

Since the beginning of her career, Rita G. had worked as a counselor for various employment agencies. Although her formal education had progressed only through one year of college, she was articulate and poised. She handled both applicants and employers efficiently enough to make a decent living.

After several years of being stuck in the same position, Rita finally began to wonder why she had not attained a spot in management. The answer came to her after a few hours of soul-searching. Rita took a long hard look at herself and faced up to the fact that she didn't have a bit of leadership ability. In fact, she had been totally overpowered by her superiors—and by fellow employees—in every job she had ever held!

No matter how well she handled customers and regardless of how hard she worked, Rita now understood that she would be dead-ended as long as her bosses eclipsed her—and took control of her. At that crucial turning point in her career, this determined woman made up her mind to *surpass* her boss in leadership strength.

Rita had recently learned of improvement through visualization. She was convinced it worked, because she had stopped smoking by using her mind to check the habit. She figured if *that* worked, why couldn't visualization bring about the basic personality changes she needed to become a strong leader?

The head of the company Rita G. worked for was one of the most confident leaders anywhere in the industry; this man handled subordinates with ease and confidence. He was able to gain total dominance over people rapidly and smoothly. In Rita's eyes, he was the most effective manager it was possible to be, so he became her perfection model. She began to intently study every one of his leadership characteristics. The anatomy of how he succeeded in commanding people was analyzed by her in fine detail—*and written down word for word.* This will give you an idea of just how thorough the personality examination was:

> Rita wrote down her observations *on a daily basis.* She watched the way her boss *moved,* studied his facial reactions when he spoke and when he reacted to things said by others. She listened to the precise words he said when dealing with employees, clients and associates. She heard and remembered the tone of his voice and the inflections that people always seemed to respond to. Rita watched every mannerism and burned every impression deeply into her mind. Before long, she was able to project herself *into his personality.* She actually began to understand exactly the way he was thinking so she could anticipate what he'd say next!

As her understanding of his leadership qualities grew, Rita created visualizations in which *she* became the boss. In these fantasies, *she* said to imagined employees the same things *he* had said, spoke in the same tone of voice *he* had used, and saw herself doing *everything* he had done to decisively lead others. In a matter of a few weeks, Rita G. felt new power flow to her. She held two sessions each week with herself—each no more than ten minutes long. But the signs were unmistakable: *the young woman was starting to take firm control of personal relationships. She was becoming a force to be reckoned with.*

Within one year from the time she decided to become a leader, Rita achieved the management job she longed for. It was done through this remarkable three-stage strategy:

1. She identified and owned up to a personal weakness.
2. She selected a perfection model who had exceptional strength in her area of admitted weakness.
3. She created visualizations that served to transfer the strengths *from* the perfection model *to her* area of personal weakness.

Tearing Down Belief Structures that Hinder You—And Building New Ones that Bring You Victory

For some unknown reason, Rita G. believed that she was unable to influence and lead others. She had probably carried this nonsense in her mind since early childhood. Perhaps one of her parents once told her that she must never attempt to assume a position of command. Possibly a teacher demanded that she suppress her aggressive tendencies. Maybe society in general beat her down. Whoever did it had repeated it often enough to establish a *belief structure* in this young woman. The structure was built as a result of *someone else's prejudices*—and had no relevance to Rita as an individual. At an impressionable age, she was led to believe that leadership was somehow wrong, so she entered the business world totally unprepared to influence others, and thus, to succeed.

The question you must be concerned about is this: What erroneous beliefs do *you* hold deep in your mind that are keeping you from reaching the prizes in life you are fully capable of having? The steel bars of these beliefs keep you hopelessly locked into a tiny cell within which your entire life will be spent—*unless you break out and start taking what is yours!*

The personal weaknesses we discussed earlier are almost always the results of faulty belief structures that were once planted in our minds. The story of Allen B., in this chapter, told of problems he had that originated during his childhood. Virtually *all* weaknesses—*all* personal shortcomings come from that same haywire programming *that does not belong inside us!*

You now possess the tools that can quickly change the belief structures which put you at the mercy of people adept at commanding others. You have one more way to create in yourself a leader of tremendous strength and magnetism. Don't forget these basic rules:

1. You must ruthlessly admit your shortcomings, fears, or any other problems that are holding you back. *Write them*

down and get them into the open. Define and isolate them from the rest of your total personality. Get to know them as well as you know your own name. If this is accomplished, you'll be able to deal with them effectively through mind control.

2. Create a visualization where you see yourself *totally overcoming* the problem. You must see yourself *excelling* in this particular area.

3. If possible, find a *perfection model*—someone who has *the specific qualities you lack.* Use this individual for the purpose of *transferring strength.* Take his or her assets for yourself! Do it by writing down every detail you observe the person saying and doing. Then, by incorporating your model's characteristics into your visualizations, you begin to take on the same strong traits.

4. Repeat your visualization at least twice each week until you start feeling changes in the way you handle yourself, then as often as necessary to bring continuing steady improvement.

Remember, the use of mind control methods to increase your influence over others is *not* necessary for your success. It is a valuable *supplementary avenue* for improving yourself, and for getting what you want quickly. The key to power through exploitation remains solidly in the area of manipulating people. The next chapter gives you a fail-safe system for taking control of every relationship you enter.

3

Using Your New People-Perception to Build Illusions of Power

A Midwest executive, head of a retail chain operation employing over 500 people, can merely enter a room and make his presence felt. Is it some kind of magic? Charisma? What *is* the mysterious aura that makes this person, and others like him, emanate such quiet strength?

The power which permeates the atmosphere around these people is *purely illusory.* It is created through the clever use of props—the same way a movie producer can use various backdrops to manufacture special effects. The fact is, if you do not become proficient at creating power illusions, you'll find it extremely difficult to progress the way you should. You will always look like a loser, or at the very best, like a borderline success. You'll find to your frustration that people far less deserving than you are moving ahead much more quickly, *because they know how to give the appearance of being strong and influential.*

This chapter shows you how to successfully play the games used by the most adept manipulators to make themselves bigger than life.

How to Set People-Traps with the Proper Bait

Not everyone is susceptible to each manipulative strategy or power illusion you'll have occasion to use. Exploitable individuals are the ones you can most easily use to elevate yourself in business or in just about any endeavor you wish to undertake. They're the ones who become the ladders by which the more aggressive people among us reach higher levels and greater prosperity.

But, if you are at roughly the same economic and social level as your adversary (or even *beneath* the level of that person), how do you go about getting control of him or her? It's understandable and plausible when an obviously affluent individual takes over people and events, but is it really possible for the average person to successfully wield that sort of strong influence? Yes! It's done by creating *illusions of power.*

These illusions are not lies or misrepresentations. They are simply the *symptoms* and *signs* of influence and power. So, by merely borrowing some of these signs from influential people, you will be able to exercise the same potent authority they do in certain important areas of life. Thus, you create various illusions about yourself which immediately bring people under your influence. This means you'll have instant and significant advantages over so-called "equals." It also means you'll be competing for advancement and recognition on even terms with people who may be much higher up the ladder than you happen to be. And equally important, it means you'll be virtually immune to people who attempt to use *you* to their own advantage.

To create illusions of power and influence, *you do not need* shiny new cars, a pretentious office, expensive clothes, or any of the other superficial trappings of success. Instead, it's *you* that really counts. It's the things you say, your reactions and your demands that make the difference.

Your skill in setting people-traps can go a long, long way toward giving you a decisive edge over others. These potent strategies follow.

How Val D. Plays the Waiting Game and Gets a Big Jump on Others

Extremely effective people-command strategies employed by Val D. have lifted him from a menial warehouse job to a top management position in only three years. His mastery of these tactics is almost certain to elevate him still further. The tactic we'll concentrate on right now is Val's remarkable but simple method for taking quick control of people by ruining their composure.

Early in his career, Val discovered that *being too available* was the mark of a fool. The more *difficult* it was to see somebody, the more *important* that somebody seemed to be. And the more important that somebody seemed to be, the more nervous the visitor was inclined to become. A nervous adversary, of course, is far easier to deal with.

Val knew that the average employee could not just wander into the office of a superior; there was usually the need for an appointment, then a wait until the boss was ready. Val also observed the same phenomenon at work in his own social life. His popularity seemed to be enormously enhanced whenever he became *less* accessible and much more "hard-to-get." Every time he declined an invitation, his social stock rose to new heights, and he was in stronger demand.

So, as soon as Val was in a position to do so, he began playing the waiting game with the people he felt would be impressed by that tactic. Certain higher-ups in the company were exempt and could see Val on short notice since he didn't want to antagonize them. But the vast majority of employees found themselves waiting to see Val, even though his "office" was nothing more than a tiny desk in a small room shared with four other employees. In most cases, he had nothing more important to do, but he made it a point to *look* as if he was struggling to solve a dozen emergencies. And when the other person finally did get in to see Val, he or she actually felt *honored!*

Now, as a top trucking company executive, Val D. has a plush waiting room outside his large office. A secretary runs this suite and asks *every* visitor to sit down and wait, whether they have an appointment or not, and every phone call for Val is automatically put on hold for awhile before he comes on the line.

The waiting game is a simple tactic and is merely one small part of his overall strategy, but it is the one Val considers instrumental to his success. He is sure it gives him a small head start toward victory in every meeting he has with another person.

Creating Obstacles that Bring You Victory

The same phenomenon that makes you a powerful factor when you are inaccessible also works when you place obstacles in a person's path. An easy conquest is simply not savored the way a hard-fought battle is, so when an individual is *gently* pushed away, *he or she will try harder and harder to get under your control.*

> That demands repeating: *An individual who is held at arm's length will fight like the devil to come under your control!*

So, why on earth would you ever want to make it easy for someone you are trying to influence? And why throw yourself at someone's feet in hopes you'll be accepted by them (a far cry, indeed, from becoming the dominant party in a relationship)? But, as ridiculous as it may seem, most people *do* make themselves easy conquests, and that's why they are in the habit of losing.

Caution: There is an *art* to creating obstacles. It's too easy to be accused of stubbornness, laziness or worse if you merely throw out excuses about why you won't go along. And, if you lay the obstacles on too heavily, the other person might feel you are too difficult to deal with and will walk away. The trick is to take *logical* and *plausible* stumbling blocks, blow them up a bit larger than they really are, then place them strategically in front of the person you wish to impress or get control of. Then you provide a bridge over the stumbling block that provides an opportunity for one more discussion. In other words, the bridge gives the other person renewed hope that everything will work out all right—despite the stumbling blocks you layed down during the initial contact.

Here's a basic example of how it works: Let's say you are interviewing for a job and competition is stiff. Aside from making a good appearance and being on your toes, there doesn't seem to be any way to rise above the other applicants in the eyes of the interviewer. But there *is* a way, and here it is:

At the conclusion of the interview, you declare that you wish to check on the reputation of the company before any decisions are made (if the firm is large and well known, you are definitely blowing a small point up to many times its usual size by subtly challenging its reputation, or at least asking about it). Tell the interviewer that you'll call as soon as your check is completed (that's the "bridge" mentioned earlier. With it, you establish the groundwork for one more important meeting with the interviewer).

You can bet that every other applicant sheepishly agreed to go home and wait for that fateful phone call. And not a single one of them expressed an interest in knowing about the company! In contrast, you made yourself a little harder to get, and rather than taking the *submissive* position of waiting for word, you take the initiative and *call the employer!* In the interviewer's opinion, *you* are the strongest applicant. Aside from that, the company representative is so curious about what your "check" will reveal, he or she *must* talk to you again.

The next case shows how dominance is attained through a variation of creating obstacles.

The Impact of "Qualifying": How Len K. Uses it to Expand His Empire

Len K. is an acknowledged master at creating illusions of power. His company has grown tremendously, almost solely on the strength of what his customers *believe*—not on what they have actually seen with their own eyes. His business consists of licensing people to offer an educational course which Len has packaged. A licensee, after paying Len a hefty fee, resides in an established territory and teaches the course to subscribers.

When he first started the business, Len attempted to *sell* his licensing arrangement to people who responded to his ads. But all the charm and logic he could muster failed to get the enterprise going. Prospects usually put Len on the defensive because his company was small, *and because they felt that Len's sales effort made his deal too easy to obtain.* So he drastically changed his approach—and immediately set about building a few illusions of power.

Len no longer sells anything. As soon as he receives an inquiry from a prospect, he begins to plant obstacles in that person's path. He establishes an entire mystique around his educational course through *challenges* put to the interested party. For example, during his initial talk with another person, Len explains that it requires a rather special background to qualify as a licensee, but then he creates a bridge by telling the individual (after hearing a little about him or her) that there is a *chance* they *can* make the grade.

At the next meeting, the prospect is noticeably relieved that Len is still interested, but then Len starts the process of further qualifying them. He puts each potential licensee through a full day of tests—then purposely takes three days to report on the results! By this time, in most cases, hopeful licensees are as ready as they'll ever be to sign on the dotted line.

So, a man who had consistently failed to get results by selling now has the ability to put people in a position where *they sell him!* No matter what you do in life, you can easily harness the power of "qualifying" to enhance your control of the people around you.

Controlling People by Asking for the Moon

If you don't make demands, you will very likely reside low on the totem pole. If you *do* make demands—but small ones—you are still in trouble. Everything you are ever willing to give another person, whether it be material or emotional, *must* be traded off for *at least* an equal share of something. This holds true whether you're a salesperson, a truck driver, a psychologist or whatever.

Very simply, the people who want the most and make that fact known get further in life. But the key thing about making demands is this: You must ask for far more than you expect to get. The result will almost always be that you receive less than you ask for, but it's much more than the quiet ones ever receive. "The squeaking door gets the oil" is absolutely true.

Here's how it works for one employee: Pete O. is a technical service representative for a machine manufacturer. He knows his job but cannot be classified as indispensible by any means. Yet, he has managed to wrangle concessions from his boss that nobody else in a similar position would ever dream of getting.

From his very first day on the job, Pete began asking for various materials that he convincingly argued were indispensible to his doing a first-rate job. It started inconspicuously with pens, note pads, an attache case and other small items. Then he jumped to an air travel card and an expense account. Now he has a company car and other valuable perquisites. The secret is that *he got his boss into the habit of giving to him.*

During all this time, Pete's fellow employees rather dumbly accepted what the job came with, and they plodded along like so many sheep. While they are certainly no less skilled at their jobs than Pete is, they have been left in the dust as far as importance is concerned, *because they have failed to create illusions of power as Pete has done so successfully!*

The more you want, the more you appear to be doing. The people who create the most commotion seem to be the most industrious, and that, you will agree, describes Pete.

Erica T's Strategy for Attaining Objectives Through Shock

Erica T. not only creates an illusion of power through making big demands, but she also uses the strategy of shock to control others. It's a two-edged sword that she wields with stunning effectiveness.

Selling commercial radio time is among the most competitive businesses in existence. There are scores of stations in any given area vying for the advertising dollars of potential clients. Erica T. sells radio time in a large eastern city, and has been at the top of the field in earnings for the past several years. This is how she accomplishes it:

First, Erica realizes that getting the full attention of her prospect is essential. The owner or manager of a business hears pitches all day, and becomes fairly immune after awhile. She knows that the only way to get full concentration is through shock tactics. This also serves to get her prospect off balance; it temporarily destroys sales resistence.

Immediately after shocking the daylights out of her potential customer, Erica presents a radio commercial schedule that represents an expenditure at least five times what the company can afford. The negotiations begin, and the woman is forced by the client to back down, finally "settling" for a sum that is actually far bigger than the average radio time salesperson would ever dream of getting from a firm of such size.

The shock tactics used by Erica are designed to provoke strong emotional responses from her prospects. Here are a few of the strategies she uses:

1. Erica introduced herself to the new ad manager of a retail hardware chain and promptly told him that his company was hopelessly far behind and old fashioned in terms of advertising and publicity.
2. She announced to the owner of a women's clothing outlet that a nearby competitor's store was so busy, thanks to radio and newspaper ads, that customers were waiting outside to get in.
3. In one instance, Erica told an automobile agency head that a rumor was going around that another neighborhood dealer was negotiating for huge blocks of broadcast time with another local radio station.

While they may often be exaggerated, Erica's shock methods all have at least substantial truth to them, and all of them put her on the side of her potential client. Thus, *she's* the one in a position to help.

This tactic will not work in every case or for every type of individual. It demands a cautious look at the prospect in terms of personality, style and spirit, and the particular shock device must not be overly offensive or insulting. But, if handled astutely, shock definitely helps you build an illusion of personal power and puts you in command of a relationship. A slightly different version of the shock strategy follows.

The Attack Defense: Dick R's Foolproof Method for Keeping the Initiative

Dick R., a salesman for an auto parts wholesaler, was well versed in all the tricks traditionally used to control customer interviews, but his main difficulties were in the non-business aspects of his life. Dick was simply unable to carry his own weight in the most basic relationships. He was controlled, used and walked on by almost everyone he came into contact with.

In the conduct of his work, Dick really did handle himself well. He consistently succeeded in getting a decisive edge over his prospects by using a strong opening offensive that put the other person on the run in terms of dominance in the relationship.

Despite this success in his job, Dick merely accepted his dismal failure as a leader away from work. For years, he never made the simple correlation between what he was doing to be successful as a salesman and how those tactics could quickly turn his private life around.

Then one day, it dawned on him: If social acquaintances, store personnel, parking attendants and everyone else in his life succeeded in pushing him around with ease, why not handle *them* just as he handled difficult sales prospects? *Why* try to be nice, easygoing or even meek when dealing with others? If they took this behavior of his as *weakness* (as most people evidently did), he intended to change his ways at once.

So, he immediately began using the attack defense that worked so well in sales: Instead of looking down at the floor when he gave his name to the hostess for a table in a busy restaurant, Dick peered deeply into the eyes of the haughty woman or man at very close range, and firmly said, "I need a table in five minutes. Last week I waited ten minutes, and two parties that arrived after I did were seated before me." At the parking lot, Dick said, "I want it parked in a spot where the doors won't be nicked, and I want it driven carefully."

The attack defense even works like a charm in Dick's social life. He lets his friends—or new acquaintances—know exactly what's on his mind without mincing words. He is *not* impolite, stubborn or arbitrary. He simply *opens* relationships with a firm statement on how he expects to be dealt with, *and he nearly always gets his way!* Not only does Dick enjoy control of others, but he enjoys respect for the first time in his life.

Using the Dark Magic of "They"

You can easily carry a board of directors around with you in your back pocket, or an attorney, an accountancy firm, or any other influential advisors you wish. They can travel with you anywhere, and come to your assistance at a moment's notice during negotiations of any description.

All unseen power sources like the ones mentioned above are "they." All carry magical clout that is rarely questioned by your adversaries. "They" has become, in the English language, a symbol for invisible forces that can change events.

Imagine yourself in a situation like the one Barbara Y. recently encountered: She had just presented a long-term lease agreement to the president of a firm that, for the past five years, had been renting an entire floor of a commercial building managed by the firm Barbara worked for. The company head was visibly upset because the new five-year lease demanded a substantial increase in rent, a reduction in the number of parking spaces allocated and a cutback in other building services. The agitated tenant began making strong arguments about why rental adjustments should be made, so Barbara promptly summoned "they."

She quietly explained to her client that the building owner's accountants and attorneys were pressing hard for even higher rentals than those he was being asked to pay. She said "they" didn't know the details of this particular lease, but if they did, would undoubtedly do everything they could to throw it away and rewrite it at much higher figures. Barbara told the man that these rentals, although steep, were still far lower than what "they" were insisting on, but that her firm's first loyalty was to trusted existing tenants.

Thus, Barbara was doing everything possible to give the man

a "break." "They" were the heavies, and the woman was attempting to protect him against these villains. He signed the lease right then and there.

There are *always* people of power behind the scenes whom you can conveniently use as "they." These nebulous figures of influence make your proposition or argument more real, more urgent and infinitely more forceful. You must make "they" sound like part of your team; as if some stern committee is waiting behind the scenes to critically examine whatever you present to them. If this is done, your adversary begins to feel rather small, and he or she senses that you hold real power—that you are the authorized representative of something much, much bigger than they had imagined at first.

"They" is created instantly when you refer to "my attorney," "my partner," "our auditing firm," and so forth. At meetings, it can help to constantly scribble notes in a pad (ostensibly, so a brief on the proceedings of the meeting can later be reviewed by your various behind-the-scenes associates).

The key element in using the dark magic of they is *never to make a decision during the first talk with another person.* As soon as you make the mistake of arriving at decisions without first consulting those created phantoms you call "they," your credibility will slide in the eyes of your adversary. The other person *expects* you to speak to your attorneys, accountants and bankers before making even the smallest move, so don't disappoint them. You must oblige and wait a day or two before deciding. In that day or two, the influence will swing strongly in your favor.

How Ray M's Incredible Rescue Scenario Brings Him Enormous Influence

Today, Ray is a well-paid vice-president of finance for a major corporation. He joined the firm only three years earlier as an accounting clerk. His tremendous climb to the top was precipitated not as much by his professional know-how as by his uncanny skill at manipulating others.

Rescuing department managers and assistant managers is Ray's strong suit. He would come along just as the other person was about to be buried in a serious expense account debacle, a budget error, a badly miscalculated sales projection or other fiscal mishap. Of course, the managers never found out that Ray himself had carefully contrived the problem. By first detecting a minor oversight (the type that is prevelent in large companies, but usually corrected by clerks), then cautiously working with the faulty figures to compound the mistake and blow it up out of proportion, Ray succeeded in slipping the noose around a few choice necks.

The corporate wheels would start turning: Ray's boss, the controller, would get wind of the problem, and begin to prepare a case against the careless but victimized manager. Such a case would definitely be embarrassing—and could sometimes even be fatal to a budding career. But, before the controller could bring heavy guns to bear on his prey, Ray was in the office of the manager "getting things straightened out". Ray had all the answers (to be expected since *he* was the one who had created the questions!) He would promise the grateful but apprehensive manager his utmost efforts to smooth everything over.

Then Ray would rush over to the controller's office and explain the slip-up in a way that made it sound insignificant. He also had the knack of making himself sound like a paragon of innocence. So, by the time he was finished, his boss was satisfied just to drop the entire mess and let Ray repair the damage in any way he saw fit. The "rescued" manager would receive another visit from Ray a few days later. The financial man would announce that it was a close call, but declare that he was successful in fixing things up. Naturally, the other person owed Ray a big one, and felt enormous gratitude—the kind that ultimately propelled him into the vice-presidency he occupies today!

Thus, coming to the rescue of another person puts you in command of the relationship. A debt is created that can never really be repaid, because it has no dollar value but does carry an enormous moral worth. The real challenge is to contrive a situation that leads your adversary to the brink of trouble, at which point you must act quickly and heroically to snatch the victim from the jaws of peril.

We are not yet finished with this crucially important subiect of building illusions of power. The next chapter is a veritable gold mine of manipulative strategies. They are the tricks which have been mastered by those people who *now have control.* Knowing them, you'll be in a position to see things more clearly than you ever have before.

4

More Dynamic Strategies You Can Use For Creating an Authority/Success Image

This chapter is oriented to things you can say and think which provide you with a look of authority and success. They are not "people-traps" as such, but lie more in the area of personal ways of doing things which are remarkably effective in giving you the edge over others.

Two Amazing Ways to Gain Hypnotic Power with Your Voice

Just about everyone imagines that the most manipulative people are loud. After all, the classic picture of the top corporate executive or any other leader is that of a glaring big shot who doesn't hesitate to shout down adversaries. How utterly wrong that conception is!

We'll talk about the pitfalls of outright abrasiveness a little later, but even the mere raising of one's voice can assure the failure of a dominant position in a relationship. Bullying is simply *not* the way to take control. What you do with your voice is one of the most important elements in attaining authority. The correct use of the voice may surprise you. Here are the secrets:

1. *Speak softly to captivate even the most difficult audience.* An unusually quiet, deliberate and precise delivery of words is a magical way to get your point across. If people have to *strain* to hear you, they'll step closer, lean toward you, or do whatever is necessary to get your message.

   In a meeting environment, your soft speech will *in-*

stantly eliminate side conversations that a more boisterous speaker invariably has to contend with. Every individual will give undivided attention.

This sort of toned-down delivery gives you an air of confidence and importance. On the other hand, the louder individual always seems to be forcing others to buy something. The shouter may succeed in temporarily startling people, but the attention this person gains quickly vanishes as the noise level becomes tiresome to others.

Practice! If you have a recorder, work on modulating the tone of your voice. Repeat sentences until they are noticeably smoother and softer. Remember to do it every time you speak in order to make it second nature.

2. *Slow down and watch your influence grow.* Machine-gun sentences can do as much to cost you influence as loudness does. Most people talk far too rapidly and the result is a poor choice of words, muddled concepts and ultimate loss of the audience.

   Slower speech gives the brain an opportunity to organize thoughts *before* you get to them. Thus, you're in a position to articulate your ideas much more clearly and effectively. Secondly, the reduced tempo of your speech gives the other person a better chance to thoroughly absorb your ideas (a *must* if you are to get control!)

   Slower speech can be mastered by more carefully measuring the things you say. *Resist the temptation to blurt out thoughts spontaneously!* Also, try to gauge what you want to say in terms of the other person's probable reaction (your knowledge of the personality types will help here). Check yourself by using the recorder, just as you do to practice speaking at lower volume.

Softer and slower speech is especially effective when you're dealing with a loud, fast-talking individual. Your calm, precise speech will eventually give you a firm upper hand in the relationship!

Silence: A Colossal Weapon in the Hands of the Manipulator

While softer and slower speech is a sure way for you to gain hypnotic power, strategic silence is a tactic certain to put you in the driver's seat. You may have observed that people involved in conversation often make observations and answer questions when they are not really prepared to do so. Out of want for anything meaningful to say, they make drab and ill-timed statements, as well as other remarks that work against their cause.

An extremely important man recently said, "Quiet people . . . those who seldom speak . . . are either very dense or very intelligent. When they turn out to be the latter, which is most often the case, I find them to be the toughest negotiators and the ablest leaders."

Strictly rationing your words accomplishes the following objectives:

1. You are listened to more intently than you would be if you spoke at every opportunity.
2. People will begin *asking you* for your opinions, and consulting you for advice. Probably because you say things more worthwhile when you talk less!
3. When you speak less frequently, it forces *your adversary* into the mistakes *you* were making when you talked too much. Now *they're* the ones who make ill-advised, badly thought out statements!
4. Silence tends to ripple another person's composure. Believe it or not, most people would be better able to tolerate a screaming, foot-stomping tirade from you than they would be able to withstand your stony silence.

Here's how one very skillful people-user makes top executives come over to her side through the use of strategic silence.

How Carrie V. Brings Important People to Their Knees

In the course of her work as a major department store buyer, Carrie V. is constantly locked in verbal combat with factory owners, international distributors and other big people in the world of merchandising.

These tough negotiations involve multiple carloads of merchandise and tens of thousands of dollars in purchase orders, so the going can get difficult. The factory owners, even though they are vitally interested in selling goods, drive the hardest bargains they can. And Carrie, despite the fact that she is anxious to submit orders, must try to save her employer every last penny she can.

Since the people she deals with are predominantly strong personalities, Carrie admits her inability to outmuscle them in a war of iron wills. She found a different way to maneuver these people, and it has proven far superior to the customary verbal shoving matches.

At carefully determined points in the conversation, *Carrie does not respond to her adversary at all.* She maintains absolute silence whenever the thing she must say is damaging to her cause! Here are some examples:

Buyer: "Remember, I told you that the discount on our last shipment of purses couldn't be repeated on future orders."

Carrie: *Absolute silence.* (Like most people, she could have answered weakly; "Yes, I remember. But I want the same discount again.")

Buyer: "I'll give you everything you're asking for on this order, but only if you'll give me a commitment for $50,000 in the next three months."

Carrie: *Absolute silence.* (If she says "yes", she's committed. But silence keeps her out of future obligations she doesn't need. So she'll say goodbye, hang up the phone, then send a purchase order a few days later. The buyer will most likely fill the order regardless of the fact that Carrie did not actually give him a verbal okay, and the man will *not* expect his further condition to be met).

Carrie's strategic silence rarely fails to swing command of the relationship to her side of the bargaining table. Every time she does it, there's an awkward pause in the discussion, and she *feels* the power flowing to her. The other party generally says something weak, just to fill the enormous void, and promptly loses the initiative.

Remember, during one of those awkward silences, the first one who speaks is the loser!

Advocacy: A Basic Key to Control over People and Events

If you take a look at the women and men who habitually control other people—and make successes of their lives—you'll see that most of them believe strongly in something. This deep belief could be in an ideal, a cause or even in a product.

The followers of the world are told what to believe in. They merely repeat a script which has been prepared for them by the true believers. These followers are awed by the people who champion causes, and they are used by those leaders. Therefore, when you become a powerful advocate of some idea or thing, *you automatically place yourself in a position of supremacy over most other human beings.*

A religious leader is a powerful advocate of a God; a star salesperson is a fanatical believer in a product or service; a political activist fervently pushes a cause. Each of these strong advocates finds it easy to gather a following.

Extreme enthusiasm is *not* a satisfactory substitute for advocacy. Neither is knowledge about a particular thing. *It has to become one of the most important parts of your life* before others will be willing to line up behind you and follow!

In one fascinating instance, a communications consultant made a moderate success of his business by simply being competent. But, when he became a strong advocate about what he believed in, he started down a fast road to wealth. Here's his story.

Martin G's Momentous Discovery, and How it Transformed His Life

If not terribly original, Martin G's business concept was basically sound. His specialty was to go from company to company, providing advice on how they could improve their communications. Martin was good at his work and had no difficulty establishing a waiting list of clients. His income was well above average, and his corporate customers usually felt that a valuable service had been rendered by the end of the visit.

But for every firm that used Martin's services, there were scores who shunned it: These unresponsive companies went about their business, while still making a mess of their communications. The consultant knew how dearly this was costing those firms, but he couldn't get through to them. The more Martin thought about his own failure to reach certain businesses, the more fervent he became about what he was doing. It was much more than simple enthusiasm; it started to become a kind of one-man crusade. The overwhelming desire to convert noncustomers to his way of thinking was burning inside him.

His first move was to condense the philosophy he felt so strongly about into a *brief* idea; one that would be immediately understood by anyone. It was this:

> *By changing all written and oral language used in a business into the simplest possible form, revenues and profits will increase because of greater understanding.*

This became Martin's credo . . . his "religion." His entire career became dedicated to the meaning in that single sentence.

Almost at once, reluctant firms began to buy his belief. They *had* to because of his incredibly strong faith in it. Business flourished as it never had before. Martin set about hiring people to assist him in consulting all the new clients, and his people followed him eagerly by virtue of the powerful ideal the man had established.

Strong advocacy can be directed to anything from a tool set

to a complicated principle. The important thing is to *believe in it with all your being!*

Note: Please don't interpret this as meaning you must become fanatical before you can take control of others. Advocacy is just *one more way* of assuming clear leadership.

Four Essential Rules for Looking the Part

This is an appropriate place to discuss rules of demeanor that will be helpful to you. No matter what your occupation is, or why you are interested in learning to control people and events, these guidelines should prove invaluable:

1. *Your general demeanor*

   Even if you are fun-loving, you must maintain a serious facade when confronting adversaries. Unfortunately, humor or banter is all too often taken by others as insincerity, lack of professionalism or flippancy.

   Smile or laugh, of course, when appropriate in response to humor by your adversary, but then get back to the matter at hand. Although it may not be totally comfortable to you, a sober manner will go much, much further in giving you a look of credibility and trustworthiness.

2. *What to do with your eyes*

   Always look squarely into the other person's eyes. There is no better way to convey a genuine sense of interest in the individual, and to show sincerity.

   Nothing will shake the faith of a person faster than someone whose eyes shift during a discussion. Inability to gaze into another's eyes is construed as weakness, and you certainly don't need an image like that!

3. *How to listen*

   At every opportunity, lean *toward* the person who is speaking. Then, when it's your turn to talk, return to your normal position. This is a marvelous trick for conveying the feeling that you are anxious to hear every word.

   Most people interrupt others, and few acts are as rude or

as inconsiderate. Try this when *you* are interrupted, even if you are in the middle of a sentence: *Stop talking* the moment your adversary cuts in! Generally speaking, the more times the other person cuts you short, the deeper they become obligated to you (unless the individual happens to be a compulsive talker who is also totally insensitive).

If you don't understand an idea or concept being described by your adversary, *ask him or her to repeat it.* There are few greater compliments than to be *listened* to! This can be a *very* effective control device.

4. *Be physically firm*

   When you shake hands, shake with *muscle.* Don't break the bones in the person's hand, but be *firm.* Avoid that limp dishrag handshake that is, unfortunately, so common.

   Stand and sit straight. Keep both feet planted solidly on the floor as if they're nailed to the spot. When standing, you can fold your hands in back of you (whatever you do, keep them out of your pockets!) When you sit, grasp the arms of the chair, just as you might imagine a king would do, or fold them on the table.

Above all, *relax,* and try to appear as if you own the place. Feel powerful and you'll look powerful!

Whenever you have the chance, *study* men and women of status and influence. Make mental notes of how they carry themselves. Even the smallest mannerisms can contribute to that extraordinary aura of strength.

Next, we'll talk about one of the oldest known ways to impress others.

Ava C's Trick for Remaining in the Limelight

Name-dropping (the strategic mentioning of important people or celebrities as personal friends) may have a dubious reputation, but one executive secretary has turned it into a fruitful tactic. Ava is constantly the center attraction at her place of employment. She's the undisputed leader of every other secretary and clerk in the company, and she's recognized by most of the executives as a first-rate power in the firm. Ava has political heft way beyond what one would normally expect of a woman in her position.

The secretary has a marvelous sense for what it takes to impress people. She learned early that respect in a large corporation comes mainly from *who you know.* Ava discovered that gaining influence wasn't a matter of working hard; it was more a question of having allies in high places. But, she also realized that she couldn't impress other secretaries the same way she turned the heads of vice-presidents. So Ava set about developing a strategy designed to work on *everyone* in the company. She intended to drop the proper names at the proper times in the proper places. This is how it worked:

> For typists, clerks, secretaries and other employees at her general level, Ava would claim the close friendship of middle management people known to, but beyond the social reach of, her fellow employees. In the minds of these people, Ava holds a handful of aces; to hear her tell it, she's on a first name basis with the personnel manager, the head bookkeeper, the sales manager and just about every other person held in awe by her equals.
>
> To the people who *own* the names she drops on her peers, Ava alleges close ties with members of the company Board of Directors. She made it a point to meet most of them on past occasions, and those fleeting encounters are all she needs to add them to her formidable list of impressive names! Middle managers, of course, never get closer to Directors than seeing their pictures in the annual report. So they have no way of knowing that Ava exaggerates the closeness of her relationships with these people.
>
> To the top brass in the company, Ava drops the names of several politicians she shook hands with once at a cocktail party. Name-dropping at this level is a trickier game because it's entirely possible that the officers of the firm *are* acquainted with senators and members of congress. But she's careful, and it has worked for over five years.

Ava makes it a point to get around. True, she meets many

people, but those introductions rarely progress beyond the initial "hello" stage.

The thing is, *she knows how to get a tremendous amount of mileage out of the names of people she meets.* And she's wise enough to know that big names really *do* mean a lot to most of us!

An important key to making name-dropping work is this: Don't use names *too far beyond* the person you are trying to impress. For example, Ava didn't attempt to mention a company director to a clerk. It would have been meaningless. Your adversaries must hear names they are familiar with, names they look up to, but names that belong to people who move about in a totally different social sphere.

It's undoubtedly true that Ava makes name-dropping work as a manipulative tactic because she really believes that she belongs in that loftier social sphere. Let's take a closer look at that phenomenon.

What "Thinking Big" Really Does for You

In the beginning chapters of this book, we went into the fascinating subject of how your mind can make you virtually anything you want to be. Reprogramming the vast unused expanses of the brain will bring about truly astonishing transformations in *any* human being. But the kind of "thinking big" we'll discuss now is different from the sweeping changes involved in rechanneling the mind. This version simply involves a different perspective on your part in certain everyday matters. Yet, simple as it is, the new perspective will do some surprising things for you.

Ava, our remarkable name-dropper, has the facility to imagine herself as the friend of some very important people. Most other people in her situation would shake hands with a senator at a cocktail party, then immediately retreat back into their rather dull existence. The reaction of the majority would be, "I was lucky to meet a famous person, but now I must hurry back to where I belong."

In stark contrast, Ava's perspective is, "I've just had the

good fortune of meeting a senator who has tremendous influence. I'll do everything I can to cultivate a relationship. After all, I'm just as worthy of position as *he* is! If that doesn't prove practical, I'll use the experience of our brief meeting to elevate myself, even if it's only a tiny notch upward from where I am now!"

Every "tiny notch upward" means something to the manipulator on the move. It is *not* usually *the big break* that gets successful people up into the top echelons of money and influence. It's the small moves, and the *cumulative effect* they have on a career or a private life.

It isn't only meeting big people that offers you the opportunity of thinking big and hitching a ride to better things in life, it's exposure to *any* new or enriching experience. Or, it can be certain *knowledge* you come upon that changes you for the better. *Collectively, these experiences should become a major force in propelling you toward the goals you desire.*

Indeed, certain types of experiences or knowledge can become *extremely* potent factors in moving you upward in life. Let's take a look at how that works for one imaginative woman.

The Impact of Intimate Knowledge: Carole P's Way of Gathering Influence

If there is one thing that will consistently command the attention and admiration of almost any other person, it is hearing something complimentary about themselves. This is doubly true when the remarks are timely and in good taste. When you possess intimate knowledge about other people, you are in a position to control them.

The negative side to intimate knowledge is gossip. This is definitely *not* the most ethical or savory way of getting control, but it is very much a part of life. And everyone who is interested in how exploitation works has to understand the way gossip is used by certain people. To deny it exists is the same as burying your head in the sand. Therefore, we'll examine its mechanics regardless of the fact that most individuals take a dim view of its use as a manipulative tactic. (The power of compliments will be thoroughly covered in the chapter about flattery, later in this book.)

In the past few pages, we discussed how information should be saved and ultimately used for advancing in life. Carole P. has made a science of it. The tidbits she collects are always about other people, specifically, men and women who belong to her social group.

Carole holds enormous influence among her acquaintances because she knows far more about every individual than any human being has a right to know. But most important, *she knows how to use this intimate knowledge adroitly.* Thus far, she has succeeded in taking undisputed control of the people in her social circle and has managed to achieve that control without seriously alienating a single one of them.

Carole *keeps a card file on every person she knows!* Every time she hears a piece of information about one of her friends, she probes until every last drop of factual meaning has been extracted. It is then entered on the card she keeps on that person. Carole does her probing subtly enough to avoid suspicion.

Her trick is this: Carole knows that in every group of people there are bound to be individuals who don't get along with certain other individuals. As a matter of fact, virtually *every* person in a group has most-favored *and* least-favored acquaintances. So when she wants to get negative information about any given man or woman, she merely goes to that person's *least-favored* acquaintance, and the gossip flows freely. Since there is very little chance that the two people in question would ever sit down and chat, Carole's nosiness remains a secret.

Then, with the veritable library of facts she has written down on each person, Carole manipulates to her heart's content. For example, she can tell a friend that a rumor is circulating that involves her, the friend. Carole tells the alarmed person that she'd be willing to put a stop to the rumor by putting pressure on a few choice (but unnamed) people in the group.

Carole's acquaintance is, of course, anxious to have the rumor halted, and with Carole's influence, nothing more is heard about it. The person is deeply indebted to Carole, and thus comes under her control a little more firmly. (This strategy is generally similar to that used in the "rescue scenario" described in the previous chapter).

Another tactic, the one most prevelantly used by Carole, involves playing people against each other in a more direct way than in the method just explained. She knows that whenever conflicts exist between two people, she can assume dominance of one by making it look as if she's joining forces against the other. Of course, she's very careful to remain scrupulously neutral, but her bits and pieces of intimate knowledge can be used to create some very misleading illusions about just whose side she is really on.

Although you may understandably balk at using intimate knowledge to control people, it is undeniably valuable to know as much as you can safely learn about the people around you.

Beware of Abrasiveness!

It has been proven beyond any doubt that abrasive people fail to progress as rapidly as those who are more mild, and more considerate of others. Abrasiveness simply gets on people's nerves, and those who practice it purposely or inadvertently are eventually stifled in their upward movement. When you are attempting to put across manipulative strategies, there is always the danger of sliding into behavior which irritates others. This warning, then, should serve to remind you of that possibility:

Keep a close eye on your adversary during the time you are attempting to take control. Watch for signs of resentment or rejection of what you are doing or saying. Some strong symptoms are:

1. A sudden decline of interest on the part of the other individual.
2. General uneasiness.
3. An increase in resistance to the ideas you put forth.
4. A flare-up of temper from the person.

When you detect any of the above signs, back off. *Repeat: Take the pressure off,* and return to as normal a relationship as quickly as you can. For the time being, *forget* the idea of gaining dominance or else you'll lose the entire ballgame.

Then, when things calm down, you can *gradually* shift back into a manipulative mode. One excellent way to cool off an overheated relationship quickly is described next.

How Milt R. Wins by Knowing When to Lose

Milt R. is an attorney. His practice is devoted mainly to negotiating personal injury settlements, and the strategies he uses to successfully bargain for substantial amounts of money can be applied by *anyone* who is interested in profits and/or influence.

In a meeting with the opposing lawyer or with an insurance company adjuster Milt makes the strongest conceivable moves to dominate the relationship. He uses fear, threats, innuendo and promises (all of which are covered in this book). In a remarkable number of instances, he is successful in winning almost everything he sets out to get for his client. It's not at all surprising, since Milt has so many weapons in his arsenal!

But, occasionally, he sees the opposition begin to slip away. Milt immediately realizes that he's on the brink of a major set-back. The adversary starts to squirm under the subtle pressure and erects defenses which makes continuing negotiations all but impossible.

At this critical juncture, Milt uses his ingenious strategy: *In the privacy of his own thoughts, he selects one point he believes important to the other person. Then he proceeds to give the opposition that single concession!* At the same time, Milt *removes* the pressure he has been exerting.

The combination of a decline in pressure and the winning of a point in the negotiations *puts the meeting back on an amicable, relaxed footing,* and Milt's adversary is lulled to sleep! Only moments pass before Milt again works his way back toward an effort to achieve supremacy, and this time, he usually *reaches* that coveted position of control. The opponent, having won once, is forever hopeful of doing it again, but while he is hoping, he is gradually *losing!*

So, don't hesitate to concede points to the other side *if* doing so puts the general relationship on ground more favorable to an ultimate triumph for you. *Just be sure that the point you decide to give up doesn't damage your overall cause.* It should be one that is far more important to your adversary than it is to you.

Making Mystery and Intrigue Work for You

In building your ability to influence and control others, a healthy dose of personal mystery can do nothing but help you. People are deeply impressed by those who operate "behind the scenes," unseen by all but a few priviliged insiders.

Even if the things you do are *not* actually deep dark secrets, they should be made to *seem* as if they are. There is nothing at all interesting about people whose lives are an open book. Why *not* create speculation about what your true purpose is? Why *not* create a little anxiety about what's *really* on your mind? Uncertainty in your adversaries will invariably work in your favor.

Most of the tactics which have been covered so far *do* help you become more mysterious in the eyes of people you deal with: *The magic of "they"* gives you an aura of intrigue. *Silence* certainly does. *Name-dropping,* if carefully handled, does too. And *being less accessible* is also decidedly mysterious.

In addition to these methods, there are several more which should go a long way toward making you a more enigmatic, and thus more desirable, personality:

1. *At every convenient and plausible opportunity, hold secret meetings, preferably behind closed doors.* If you work in a company environment, for example, this is certain to make at least a dozen key people wonder what's going on. The meeting itself might be as innocent as a discussion about the weather, but a few folks will be sure it's a momentous summit meeting. Your status will grow in direct proportion to your reputation for intrigue!

2. *Make it a point to spend some time off, and keep your whereabouts secret.* This is perhaps the boldest intrigue-builder of them all. Both business associates and friends will wonder for days afterward what you were up to. And, if you are successful at withholding the answer, their imaginations will have you performing all sorts of high-level functions, even if you spent the time basking at the seashore. This can be devastating when subtly combined with name-dropping!

3. *Say much, much less about what you do and think.* Remember the fact that the less information you impart to others about your business, the more people will have to guess about. And, if you make them guess, they will almost always overestimate and overreact. When they behave that way, you will be built up to magnificent proportions!

One eminently successful manipulator said, "I wish I was as rich and powerful as everyone *thinks* I am!" That neatly sums up the impact of mystery and intrigue.

Now it's time to get into a discussion about the heavy guns of manipulation. The background you now possess will set the stage for your rapid understanding of the following extraordinary people-control tactics.

5

How to Zero-In and Get Quick Control Over Your Adversary

Legends tell us that when conflicts occurred in the Old West, the fastest gun most often emerged the winner. Taking the initiative seemed to be the main objective, if not a life or death necessity. So it is in controlling others. You'll have significantly more success *in everything you do* if you take firm steps in gaining dominance over the individual you want to deal with, *and your success will be magnified if that dominance is attained rapidly.*

This chapter is intended to give you some very effective ways to get the initial jump on adversaries. It also shows you how to block the other person from getting a grip on *you* during the early stages of a relationship. These tactics give you the means for remaining just out of the other person's reach, while you are busy strengthening *your* hold on him or her!

Taking the First Big Step to Absolute Command Through the "Don't Like Me . . . Follow Me" Approach

The pattern you are able to establish *in the first few minutes* of meeting a new individual will, in almost every case, set the tone for all future dealings. It's extremely difficult to change pace after you have conveyed a first impression, so you should try to avoid entering new relationships with an attitude of, "I want to be your friend, and therefore I'll do anything within reason for you." That is pure poison!

Many employees have that attitude toward the boss, and many individuals just entering new social groups or environments are likely to be thinking that way. The employer has every reason to believe that this particular employee is totally lacking in leadership qualities and will stand for being exploited constantly. The people in the social group regard such people as part of the scenery, followers who never have anything worthwhile to say.

The fact is, it is far better to be faced with the necessity of *toning down a too-powerful initial impression* than it is to try to convince people that you are not really as weak as your first impression led them to believe. When you knock people off their feet upon first getting acquainted, they at least consider you colorful and interesting, and that is *far* more favorable than having them think you're a follower!

Getting quick initial control goes further than just putting you in command of another person; *it also exposes you to a vast number of opportunities that the average person never sees or hears about.* Here's how that works.

When powerful and influential people are in group situations, they often look for strength in others. But what they most frequently see is that same weakness we spoke of before (the "please like me" attitude). On those rare occasions when they *do* observe manipulative qualities in others, *they are drawn to it as if to a magnet!*

This is where life's golden opportunities come from. *This* is what is meant by "being in the right place at the right time". The strong person is discovered and is offered chances to be at the top, because *he or she demonstrated the ability to control people and events!*

Let's take a close look at a group of proven tactics that do the job of getting you control within the first few minutes of a new relationship.

Maury L's System for Getting a Quick Grip on the Reins of Leadership and Influence

Maury is the first one to admit he possesses no special social abilities or knowledge. Yet he has rapidly risen to a position near the top of the entertainment industry. He is executive vice-president of a major broadcasting network.

When he was just beginning his career with the company in a

low-level job, Maury realized that *all the job know-how in the world would not, in itself, assure his success.* There were scores of people in the firm vying for positions of higher income and prestige, and most of them knew more than he did about the business.

More significantly, *these other ambitious employees were quick on the trigger,* just like the Old West gunfighters mentioned before. They had the knack of turning on the charm to rapidly captivate others. Time and time again, Maury found himself excluded from "the inside circle of power," because his competition moved faster than he did.

The young executive *had* to develop a way to get fast control of new acquaintances if he was to survive in the entertainment business. He ruled out charm as a possible method because he knew his competition was better at it, and probably always would be. After giving the problem careful thought for several days, this is the plan Maury created, the one that was to eventually help propel him to a vice-presidency:

> *Upon first meeting any new employee, prospective employee or client of the company, Maury would make a commitment to help that person in any way he could.* This was done *before* his more socially skillful competitors got their grips on the new person.
>
> This pledge to assist was made despite the fact that Maury was still a comparatively low-level employee in the firm. His sincerity, reenforced by a hearty handshake and an arm around the shoulder of the other person, seemed to make up for his lack of rank.
>
> The individual was made to feel important, and from that moment on, looked to Maury for advice and moral support. This was true *even though his fellow employees outcharmed Maury!* It was apparent that our friend's desire to assist new acquaintances meant much, much more to those people than mere personality or social dazzle!

This phenomenon did not escape the notice of Maury's superiors in the company. They saw the man become a focal point for both subordinates and higher executives, and they noticed he was acceding to this strong leadership position *without the need of giving lavish parties or other social favors!*

This powerful quick-control strategy is *far different* from the attitude of "I want to be your friend, and therefore I'll do anything within reason for you" mentioned earlier in this chapter. Let's take a look at just how different Maury's tactics are from that statement of weakness.

Three Conversational Tricks that Demand Immediate Respect and Attention

You can easily use the three essential elements in Maury's quick-control strategy. In the very brief moments you have available to get a grip on your adversary, you can cover each one of these vital points:

1. "*We have to pull together*"

   Let the other person know that it takes a *team effort* to make progress, and express your total willingness to cooperate with the individual in any way you can (within the authority of your position).

   This approach makes plenty of sense to a newcomer who is bright enough to realize that *no one person* can or should promise everything. So your statement is perfectly plausible. It is also impressive because of its unselfishness. In the eyes of others, you are *not* simply looking after your own interests, and you are *not* displaying weakness by laying at the feet of the person and begging to be accepted!

2. "*I'll do what I can*"

   You then emphasize the fact that you'll do *only what is within your power to accomplish.* This is in extreme contrast to the insincere things people usually hear, like, "Don't worry about *anything,* I'll take care of it."

   Again, Maury's words have a clear ring of truth, especially when compared to the wild promises that will soon be made by his rivals. Your new acquaintances prefer a *meaningful* vow of help from someone who might have limited influence but *admits* it!

3. *"When we get down to serious matters . . ."*

The final step in this quick-control strategy is a subtle attack on the phony charm that will inevitably gush from your competitors as soon as they get a chance to meet new employees or clients. You can take most of the impact out of the charm *before* it actually comes. Simply make the point that this get-together (whatever the occasion happens to be) will bring out the phoniness in some people, and that *nothing of importance will be discussed until a later, more appropriate time.*

Thus, your rivals are effectively stopped in their tracks. Equally important, *you have neatly set the stage for a later visit with the person.* This later date will be the time when you can get down to brass tacks *without* the distraction of your competition tugging from all sides!

Surrounding Yourself in Mist: How it Gives You an Immediate Edge in the Control Game

The rest of this very important chapter is devoted to other ways you can seize quick initiative in one-on-one relationships. But first, we'll discuss a method to be used in protecting yourself from manipulation by others. As we go into these various quick-control tactics, you'll see that *the "spotlight" should always be focused on your adversary.* It's as if two people are on stage, and the circle of brilliant light flashes first on one, then on the other. The one who spends the most time in the light *will almost always be the one who loses control,* as you will see later.

So how do you remain *out* of the glaring and power-stealing light? One of the very best ways is to *be a mystery to other people.* The less your adversaries know about you, the more powerful they think you are! A common mistake people make is to talk themselves right into the hands of others! These men and women practically *dive* into the spotlight.

Work on answering direct questions with vague, *unrevealing* responses. Don't say any more about what you do and what you are really like than you absolutely have to.

Work on keeping conversations *centered on your adversary.* That keeps the spotlight *off you!*

Doing these things will shroud you in a mist that most people will not be able to see into. This gives you an aura of mystery which is *exactly the way you want other people to see you!* Unfortunately, those who are easy to "read" are often the easiest people to control. Being mysterious will probably result in making you somewhat *quieter* (but being quieter will *not* get in the way of your gaining personal power). You'll find out eventually that *the most influential people are frequently the ones who say the least.*

Now we can move on to the most successful quick-control tactics available to expert people-handlers.

Getting Your Adversary to Make the First Move

Putting that infamous "spotlight" on the other person is one of the vital first moves in taking quick control. You will protect yourself tremendously by hiding in the mist just described. But at the same time, you have to make sure that the circle of light envelopes, and remains focused on, your adversary. This is your main objective:

> *Get the other person to come out and tell you what's on his or her mind.*

The most successful negotiators in the world are those who manage, through various manipulative tactics, to get their opponents to lay their cards on the table face up!

In any confrontation, as soon as you are able to learn what the other individual is after, you can usually get anything you want! Here's an example of how this works:

Imagine you are an outstanding college athlete, and you have been approached by a pro team. The recruiter for the club will want to know how much money you are willing to sign for. First of all, if they can get you to *mention* a low figure (one *below* what they originally and secretly planned to offer you) they'll naturally present offers around that sum in hopes of getting your agreement.

The athlete who also happens to be a clever negotiator will *immediately* start asking the recruiter how much his best players currently receive. He'll insist on knowing this *before* he gives any answers and lays his own cards on the table. This might seem obvious, but it's a basic strategy in getting control, one that is completely forgotten in an amazing number of cases.

The party who first lets a figure slip out is the loser.

Money isn't the only area to consider. Getting the first commitment works just as well in job interviews, in sales, in social relationship and in practically any person-to-person situation where one will ultimately win and one will come in second.

Four case histories follow. Each one illustrates for you a different method to be used in getting commitments without first giving them. Remember, they are the *cornerstones* of your manipulative skill, because *they give you the initial advantage in a relationship* which you must possess in order to come out ahead!

How Howard L. Gets Commitments Without Giving Them, Through the Two-Step Laundered Feedback Method

Howard is a successful city official and is rising rapidly in the opinion of political experts in his community. They feel he'll be a strong contender in the next mayoral election. One of the young man's greatest skills is his ability *to extract solid commitments from people in exchange for a lot of words that sound good to his adversaries, but don't really amount to anything they can put their fingers on.*

That is no simple trick, especially when you consider the fact that Howard deals with some high-powered people who are skillful manipulators in their own right. The men and women Howard uses are accustomed to receiving concessions and favors in return for their influence and efforts. But when they deal with this particular city employee, they usually seem to walk away empty-handed.

The technique Howard employs to accomplish this is called "laundered feedback." These steps explain how it works:

1. When Howard first meets with an individual or a group for the purpose of granting political favors in return for votes, he opens by making a statement to this effect:
   "Let's be totally open with each other. I want to know *exactly* what's on your mind, and I want *you* to know exactly what my position is. Now, tell me what you would like."

The politician has done *two* things. He has, of course, invited the other person to speak first (which puts that individual at a clear disadvantage), and he has disarmed the other side by professing his desire to be perfectly open and straightforward. In a moment, we'll see just how "open and straightforward" Howard actually is!

2. Howard's adversary generally begins the conversation by describing what is wanted from the city—or from Howard personally. The politician listens carefully, and while he is listening, *he is preparing "laundered feedback" in his mind.*

Laundered feedback is simply an *instant replay* of what the other person has just said. When the adversary hears his own views being repeated by Howard, he believes that the politician *shares his convictions*, and will therefore do everything possible to help! This brief example shows how the replay works:

A retail department store chain owner came to Howard in an effort to get improved street lighting in certain areas near his various outlets. As soon as the man completed his plea, Howard went right into an emotional speech about the sad state of commercial lighting in some parts of the city. *Howard had actually repeated exactly what the man had said only moments before* (with just a few words changed around)! By laundering the feedback in this way, he made it sound as if *this particular problem was the most important issue of his entire career,* and the retailer walked out of Howard's office *convinced* that he had a solid commitment from the city official!

The fact is, Howard gave *no* commitment in this instance and rarely does in others. His secret to staying out of burdensome obligations (while getting others deeply *into* them) *is by feeding their words back to them.* But before they are fed back (or replayed), the person's words are *laundered* by Howard; they are decorated with his brand of sincerity, emotion, or whatever else it takes to create the illusion *that he shares, just as passionately, his adversary's point-of-view!*

Kelly T's Question-Answer: Her Simple Trick for Getting and Keeping the Initiative

In the field of precious gem sales, one can rarely succeed without first acquiring the ability to command relationships with clients. And since most prospective buyers are people of at least moderate affluence, this can sometimes be a challenge.

When Kelly T. was just getting started in the business, she found herself immediately losing control of every potential customer. Interviews went smoothly during her introduction, and through the small-talk phase she used to "break the ice." But, the moment she shifted the conversation over to the subject of rare stones as an investment, things started downhill. In just minutes, Kelly would realize that any chance she had of getting an order was gone forever.

For weeks, she pondered the possible reasons for this sudden deterioration in her presentations. Kelly reconstructed every interview, and searched for some common thread that might reveal the weakness that was keeping her from high earnings. She finally found it. Kelly realized the fact that *as soon as the conversation changed from pleasantries to business, her adversary began to pump a steady stream of questions at her!* Kelly, in an effort to be helpful, answered them. Then, 10 or 15 minutes later, the prospect would thank her and be on his way without giving her an order. She had served as an information source that would help the investor in his future dealings, but had failed miserably in her own cause!

Thus, the "question answer" tactic was adopted by Kelly. In all future interviews, she would *tightly manage the facts* given to prospects and she would retain command by *never allowing herself to be put in the positon of a simple "giver of answers."* From that point on, *every* question asked by a prospect, no matter what it happened to be, would be answered by Kelly *with a question of her own.* Here are a few examples of how she does it today:

Prospective Buyer:	"What is your approximate price range for white, medium-grade one-carat diamonds?"
Kelly:	"How many are you planning to purchase?"

A straight answer from Kelly (which she was accustomed to giving in the recent past) would have severely damaged her strength. But in the above example, she begins to evaluate the shopper's intent to buy and moves him a little closer toward a close.

Here's another typical "question answer" she uses successfully:

Prospective Buyer:	"Do you have any kind of payment terms available for investments like these?"
Kelly:	"If you can give me an idea about how much cash you can conveniently lay out initially, I might be able to come up with a plan."

Her earlier answer would have been a standard yes, no or maybe. But now Kelly gives the ball right back to her adversary (very definitely a version of getting *out of* the spotlight, as discussed earlier). She uses *his question* to dig out vital information that is usually of enormous help in getting the sale!

No matter how curious the other person is, and regardless of how hard they try to get Kelly to answer the questions, *they find themselves on the answering end instead* or, in other words, on the defensive. The woman gets a quick upper hand in almost every presentation she makes, and her sales have skyrocketed as a result.

The following tactic is one more very good way for you to rapidly seize and hold the initiative.

Establishing a Command-Response by Using "Micro-directives"

The most effective manipulators not only use the previously described devices to get rapid control of relationships, but they also work very hard to establish a *command-response* at the very beginning of a social or business association.

A command-response is simply the process of *getting your adversary accustomed to taking orders from you.* Put another way, *the other individual is conditioned to expect commands from you.* Establishing a command-response is crucially important to you for two reasons:

1. If *you* become identified as the one to issue directives, then your adversary automatically becomes the one who *follows* them. It's *exceedingly* difficult for the subservient member of a relationship to suddenly take a dominant position. Therefore, the party who succeeds in first setting up a command-response is invariably the winner.
2. When you get into the practice of conditioning others to expect commands from you, it becomes habit. This quickly turns into leadership power which you soon wield as a matter of second nature.

But the problem is, you can't very well meet a new person for the first time and start giving orders to that individual! There's no faster way to create antagonism. Therefore, you have to build a command-response in a *subtle* way. To do this, you use *micro-directives* at the very beginning of a relationship.

A micro-directive is technically a command, but it is actually a request so small and insignificant that hardly anyone would ever *consider* it a command. A micro-directive might come in any form, including these:

1. Would you please reach over and get me the menu from that table?

2. Could you call Shirley and tell her to expect us this evening?

3. Would you mind closing that door when you pass by it?

They are innocent requests, asked politely and respectfully. But when a new relationship is peppered with a dozen or two of them, *these micro-directives make the influence flow directly to the party who is issuing them!* The other person doesn't really comprehend the phenomenon that is taking place, but he or she can *feel a change in the power balance within the first 30 minutes of the new relationship!*

Let's take a look at the way a small business operator uses the power of micro-directives to make her life easier and more profitable.

Martha F's Fabulous Skill at Assuming Immediate Leadership over New Friends and Clients

Martha owns and operates a temporary help agency. It's a brutally competitive business, made even more difficult by pressures from client companies and job applicants. If there was ever a situation where manipulative skills are mandatory, this business is it. Martha admits she wouldn't last a week without the ability to use others. "I'd be pushed around by nearly everybody I come into contact with," she claims. "But because I have developed the talent to give orders, *I'm* the one who does the pushing when it's needed."

The agency owner uses micro-directives *from the first*

moment she makes a new acquaintance. The following rundown illustrates how she consistently handles both job seekers and personnel directors with large firms:

With applicants who call her for jobs, Martha establishes a pattern of command through micro-directives. It's carefully woven through the fabric of her relationship with the individual *so there's absolutely no question about who's boss!* These are the key elements:

When a job hunter calls, Martha begins, as you would expect, by asking for the person's name and address. But then she asks for a detailed work background which, invariably, the applicant doesn't have committed to memory. She counts on this, since it makes the person do a little work to conform to her wishes, and effort like that helps out Martha in a dominant role.

Next, the individual is instructed to come to Martha's office for a personal interview. During this visit, the applicant is asked to verify school graduation dates, to provide references and so forth. These are micro-directives, and there are at least 20 others scattered throughout the meeting. *Each one puts Martha a little more firmly in control!*

The agency operator does it *no differently* when dealing with top-level personnel officers in major firms. While her overall manner is flawlessly proper, the power-packed micro-directives are still there, giving Martha that subtle edge.

She'll ask the personnel manager for formal data about what the company's business is. She'll request information about key management people, about wage levels, about facilities on the premises and more. The company representative finds himself *spending time and effort to oblige Martha's requests,* and he also discovers that the woman has quietly achieved the upper hand!

The next time you have the opportunity, try a sprinkling of micro-directives. Don't be surprised if they become steps to supremacy over the other person!

6

Getting Who and What You Want Through the Potent Strategy of Downgrading

The first *major* manipulative tactic we'll explore is *downgrading*. It qualifies as an important exploitive tool for two reasons: (1) it is very widely used in controlling people, and (2) it *works!*

Downgrading, and the other major manipulative tactics which follow in later chapters, have one characteristic in common. *They must be used with a considerable degree of delicacy because they penetrate very deeply into human emotions.* Small doses go a long, long way, and overdoses can easily blow up in your face. Therefore, it is far wiser to use the major tactics sparingly *until you are absolutely sure of what their impact will be on any given person.*

One more characteristic that is exclusive to the strategies of *downgrading, flattery, fear* and *promises* is that many individuals are reluctant to use them in winning people-to-people confrontations. Those who remain hesitant to use them severely reduce their chances of ever taking leadership positions. For this reason, the remaining chapters are filled with case histories which illustrate just how simple it is to use the major tactics. If you can't at this point imagine yourself wielding fear or practicing downgrading to take control, those stories are likely to change your thinking and the course of your life!

The Amazing Treadmill Phenomenon

As soon as an individual becomes satisfied, that person's desire to work almost always begins to erode. That means, if you happen to be a boss who wants to get the most out of your people, you should never tell them how well they are doing. In theory, that's just the way it has to be. But the trouble is, if you *never* give your employees a good word about their efforts, they will eventually become discouraged. A lack of praise and recognition is very tough on people, and not many of them will tolerate such an utter lack of responsiveness on the part of the top person. So the answer is to create a treadmill that permits you to give praise for exceptional effort, yet keeps the worker toiling *in the same spot* (see illustration, page 100). In other words, the person remains in place on your treadmill no matter how often you acknowledge a job well done.

Here's how such a phenomenon is created: When you pat people on the back from time to time (which you realize must be done to keep them happy), you should have a way to yank them back to their spot on the treadmill. That's where downgrading enters the picture. It quickly *erases* the advantage you hand a person when you tell him how great he's doing. But, if handled adeptly, *downgrading doesn't depress or deflate the ego of the individual.* It merely brings things back to neutral—where you want them. Your objective is to keep your adversary at a specified point on your treadmill. You *advance* the individual through praise (manipulation by *flattery* is covered later), *but you bring him or her back to that desired point through downgrading.*

How to Keep Employees on the Treadmill

A. Try not to let an individual get this far back on your treadmill. Too much downgrading and too little recognition will push him back to this position. Your adversary begins to feel worthless, and eventually starts to perform that way.

B. This spot on your treadmill is where people should spend the most time. You can advance them slightly through a positive tactic like praise (as you should every now and then), but be careful not to let them slip over the edge!

C. This is as far as you should let your adversary advance. Let him spend a little time here, then get him back to the starting point through downgrading.

D. *Too much* recognition and your adversary suddenly feels too strong to be dominated by you. *Don't* let them get this far (unless you are ready to be controlled by them).

You can now see that downgrading will *not* work as a tactic by itself. Alone, it can only antagonize people. It *must* be used in close conjunction with a *positive* force like praise or recognition.

By the same token, praise and compliments will not work by themselves either. These positive forces will push your adversary off the top of the treadmill, and when that happens, he goes out of your sphere of influence. Therefore, *successful* manipulation demands that you dispense almost *equal doses of positive and negative.* Downgrading and praise should offset each other.

How Jerry L. Fine-Tunes People by Playing "Set-Up/Knock-Down"

Jerry is the head of a small public relations firm. He uses downgrading to control both his staff and his clients. The game he plays so adeptly is called, in his own words, "Set-Up/Knock-Down." "There's no way I can keep people in precisely the position I want them without using a combination of compliments and criticism," explains Jerry. "I realize that not everyone wants to operate that way, but it works beautifully for *me*."

Jerry has perfected the skill of *fine-tuning* the men and women he works with through his method. He's an excellent judge of character, *and* a perceptive observer of where a particular individual is on the spirit scale at any given moment. Fine-tuning works this way: If a certain employee or client is difficult to handle because of some temporary feelings of self-importance, Jerry wastes no time in *knocking that person down* a few pegs through downgrading. In just a moment, his adversary is placed in a far better position to deal with.

At the same time, Jerry occasionally encounters people in low spirits. This is every bit as detrimental to his cause as excessive spirits, so he *raises* the individual on the spirit scale for a long enough time to establish his point.

The trick is in delivering just large enough a dose to get the job done. Too much or too little can work against Jerry. For example, he recently sensed that a member of his staff was overly elated with himself. This man has just landed a sizable account for

Jerry's firm which was fine, but the triumph made this individual rather cocky. Thus, Jerry found he was having trouble getting through to his man, so the company owner merely had to bring his employee down to earth. It would, in his estimation, take a delicately delivered personal blow. So Jerry called the man into his office and explained that a single victory like the one he had just achieved did *not* by any means make a season. "It takes continuing effort like that to be considered productive," Jerry told him. *His man instinctively lost that defensive edge he had been carrying around with him since the big account had been landed.* Jerry regained control of the relationship, and everything was nicely brought back into perspective.

It's possible that downgrading of the kind used by Jerry will cause an adversary to sink in spirits—perhaps for the reason that he or she thinks extraordinary efforts are going unappreciated. *You must train yourself to have the sensitivity to see such a drop in spirits!* Then you'll be able to *fine-tune* through positive tactics like compliments.

The next section illustrates a way in which it is possible *to both downgrade and uplift at the same time.*

"You're Great, But . . ."

"But" is a magic word. It lets you legitimately *contradict* a statement you made just a moment earlier! In the potent strategy of downgrading, it's a word you must use generously. "Your performance has been remarkable, and you're heading toward tremendous success. But, there are several problems that might hold you back. I feel we can overcome those problems if I can get your total cooperation." These words were used by a master manipulator to get control of another person.

The "but" always modifies the original statement. The original statement may be either positive (complimentary) *or* negative (downgrading). If the original statement is negative, the strategy has more shock value. For example:

"The quality of your work has recently been far below what I expected from you, *but* I feel confident that it can be corrected if I can get you to do exactly as I say."

The first part of the sentence can be just about as drastic as you want it to be *if* a positive statement *follows the "but."* On the other hand, if the *positive* statement is first, the negative downgrade which follows must still be rather delicate. The reason for this is simply that it is always the *last* statement which is most clearly recalled by your adversary! The parting shot is the most potent one, and you do *not* want to leave the other person down-in-the-dumps unless there's a very good reason to do so. So use "but" freely to fine-tune the people in your life. Just remember to use the negative *first* if a splash of cold water will be beneficial to your cause. Then follow with an uplifting statement. Most important, make every effort to evaluate your adversary in terms of how high he's flying at that crucial moment. This will tell you exactly how strong your positive and negative declarations should be.

Selecting the Best Shot: Beth F's Uncanny Method for Getting Control

Beth F. is considered by her peers to be a dominant personality. She has that tremendous magnetism that people can sense the moment she enters a room. She's distinctly a leader in a field where the leaders are among society's most influential and affluent people. Beth is a top newspaper reporter.

Downgrading gets Beth interviews that other reporters fail to get. For example, a celebrity is more likely to give her a statement if confronted with news that his popularity is slipping. A usually aloof professional athlete is more apt to talk to Beth when she tells him he is no longer hot news. But Beth *cannot* use downgrading in her job without first considering the impact it will have on the other person. Here's how she does it:

She pegs her adversary in terms of sensitivity. Beth understands that extremely sensitive people are especially susceptible to downgrading. They place tremendous importance on what other people think of them, they need the respect and esteem of others and they are shattered by criticism. Thus, downgrading is *super*-effective on the more sensitive individuals among us, *but a little downgrading goes a long, long way with them!* Beth has found that women, as a rule, are more sensitive than men, so she automatically handles them more gently.

Another general rule is, the more "rugged" Beth finds a person, the better they can absorb her blows. While judging by appearances or first impressions is an imperfect way to handle people, it still gives the reporter good results. She has become very adept at estimating a person's sensitivity by the way he or she dresses, speaks and reacts. In Beth's experience, more refined and softer spoken people are the most sensitive ones (although she has found exceptions to this.)

Remember, as a reporter, Beth must constantly get the upper hand in relationships—and do it quickly. In her work, there isn't sufficient time to study people in order to appraise them. *Decisions have to be instantaneous and accurate.* Therefore, by necessity, she "shoots from the hip" in sizing people up. These fast appraisals, Beth admits, are risky. If *you* have the luxury of time to make people judgements, *you'd be better off going a little more slowly than she does!* Still, the woman claims to have better than an 80 percent accuracy factor. And she's sure that this uncanny success has been instrumental in her eminence as a reporter.

Four Perfect Downgrading Targets for Guaranteed Success

Let's carry the refinement of downgrading as a manipulative strategy to the next stage. There are four ideal situations which create excellent opportunities for downgrading. They are summarized for you here, then described in detail in the following pages:

1. *In the process of recruiting, downgrading is an indispensable tactic.* When you are involved in the delicate process of bargaining for an individual's services at the lowest possible price, you *must* have a way to *devalue* that person's talents without wrecking the relationship. *Downgrading* is the answer.

2. *In maintaining control of people,* there are few strategies

as useful as downgrading. The essentials have already been covered, but here's one more reminder: the *quickest way to bring a person down a few notches is through downgrading.* And as soon as they've been pulled back down to solid earth, you'll find it far simpler to deal with them!

3. *Whenever you find yourself in a situation of hard negotiating, downgrading will get you the best possible deal.* What other method do you have at your command which permits you to budge a seller who considers his or her product or service indispensable? It's almost the same tactic used in recruiting, but instead of devaluing a *person's* estimation of himself, you are devaluing *an object* you want to possess at a lower price.

4. *In getting yourself into more important and higher paying positons,* downgrading might be all you'll ever need! A case history at the end of this chapter relates a remarkable system for getting big salary increases. It was discovered by an employee *purely by accident,* but he swears that there is simply no better way to get started on a ladder to success *and no surer way to keep climbing!*

Now let's explore these astonishing tactics more closely.

Getting Super Recruiting Results with a New Version of the Carrot/Stick Game

In obtaining the services of other people in money-making causes (whether you are recruiting on behalf of an employer, or for yourself), you will frequently observe that people place themselves high above their real spot on the ability scale in order to get better jobs and/or more pay. A tremendous amount of exaggeration takes place at employment interviews.

As the recruiter, you must possess a means to strip away that bravado. In fact, even if the applicant's attitude of self-importance is *true,* you should have a way to bring the individual back to a position where he or she will be easier to negotiate with.

There is no more difficult task than to strike a bargain with someone who has an inflated estimation of himself.

But the problem is that simple downgrading is sometimes too harsh a tactic to use in the process of recruiting; your adversary probably hasn't met you before, and therefore might be insulted by even a mild dose of downgrading. Besides, you really don't *know* the person well enough to accurately select areas in which he might be vulnerable to downgrading. So the "carrot/stick" plan works best in recruiting. This is how to do it:

Every time your adversary attempts to establish himself or herself as a master in a particular area, you *immediately* explain that *others* who have worked for you in the past have *failed* in that certain job, but that you would generously reward the person who could, indeed, make a success of it. This neatly puts the applicant in a positon of *having to prove an alleged ability to you.* He or she understands right off that *bragging is meaningless.* It's *performance* you want to see, and you will *not* pay big wages until the job is done *the way you demand it be done!*

As you can see, your downgrading is directed against *another person* (your former employee in this case) and your adversary can't possibly take offense at that. Plus, the applicant has trapped himself; he has already *claimed to be an expert* in an area or areas of your business, so he can't very well come out later and say something like, "How can I *wait* for financial rewards if I might have trouble performing that certain job?"

The "carrot" is the reward, the "stick" is what you use to hold the reward out in front of your adversaries to keep them running for it. It works *very* effectively in recruiting, especially when combined with the downgrading of an unknown third person, as this example has illustrated.

Ned C. Describes How "Like/Dislike" Keeps 75 People Under Control

Ned is national sales manager for an office machine manufacturing company. At any given time, he has a field sales organization of around 75 people all over the country. The problem of keeping tight reins on an organization this large and spread out is monumental. He tried frequent written communications, contests which provided valuable gifts for good performance, publicity about deserving individuals in the company newspaper and many other methods to keep morale and loyalty high. But there was something missing. Ned admitted there was a lack of punch in his leadership. His relationships with men and women in the field were somehow flat.

The sales manager finally realized what was needed: He was indeed the boss *in title,* but he really possessed no power. Ned actually did not have a way to make an *impact* on his people. True, he could issue orders, reprimands and encouragement, but these were emotionless exchanges that Ned felt were forgotten as soon as he and the other person went their own ways.

A very good way to bring emotions into his relationships, Ned reasoned, was to *introduce more like/dislike between himself and each of his salespeople.* The "like" was already present; it was the encouragement and praise he had been dispensing rather freely—but to no avail. He was sure he now needed a "dislike" factor, a way to occasionally get under the skin of a person to make that individual temporarily dislike him. Ned was sure this would accomplish two objectives:

1. It would make his encouragement and praise much more meaningful to his people.
2. As mentioned before, the use of carefully handled downgrading *would* make just about any salesperson dislike Ned for awhile, *but it would also trigger emotions in that person.* And Ned was positive that once he reached that "hot button," he could take control of the relationship!

So the manager started prodding his people. Now, every time he spots a vulnerability, he jabs. When he senses the ire rising dangerously close to the boiling point, he cajoles and soothes his adversary. Ned manipulates his big sales force with the same ease with which an adult handles a child.

Instead of being taken for granted, a compliment from Ned

is now regarded as the most treasured possession a salesperson can own (next to a fat cash bonus). The men and women under his command *value his esteem and fear his bite!*

Jackie V's Fabulous Bargaining System

Jackie V. estimates that in the course of a typical year, *she spends 20 percent less money* than the average person making identical purchases! Jackie's trick is to downgrade the products she wants to buy, thus forcing the prices down. When shopping for large items like automobiles, major appliances or other "big ticket" merchandise, it works like a charm for Jackie. In the course of conversation with the salesperson, *she finds vulnerabilities in the item—the same way a manipulator detects weaknesses in a human being.*

A washing machine might be missing a feature she wants; a car invariably has minor design flaws; a new outfit might be a slightly different color than she had in mind. *Whatever* the problem happens to be, Jackie uses it as a wedge to weaken the seller's position. The woman never shops in stores where prices are not subject to discount. Jackie must have assurance that her salesperson has the authority to drop the price for her. Knowing that, she proceeds to undermine the suitability of the product—regardless of the fact that she wants to buy it!

This strategy also depends on a *combination of praise and downgrading;* devaluation by itself will succeed only in convincing salespeople that you are merely insulting a certain product. But if you express desire for, say, the washing machine, then you *can* successfully criticize various things wrong with it. For example;

> "This is *exactly* the size, color and brand I've been looking for. If it only had a permanent press cycle!"

The stronger Jackie's desire for an item, the more vehement she can make her fault-finding; the more insistent she is that the problem is a major obstacle, the more likely it is that the clerk will eventually cave in on price! Her strategy works on just about every kind of purchase except groceries.

Dick L's Unbeatable System for Getting Big Promotions and Salary Boosts

Dick could scarcely tolerate his job. He was a shipping department assistant and spent his days wrestling heavy crates onto truck tailgates. He handled this menial work well but couldn't disguise his unrest. The shipping department supervisor finally asked the young man what his problem was, and Dick came right out and expressed his feelings about the work. He made no attempt whatsoever to spare anyone's feelings since he no longer cared whether he was fired or not.

So, in effect, Dick told his boss that he thought the job was beneath him. While it definitely had given him a start, he explained, it was no longer a challenge, since he felt he was capable of much more responsibility. Dick's next statement was going to announce his intention to quit the firm, but he never got it out. *The supervisor put the unhappy young man in charge of a small section of the warehouse!*

In thinking about this startling turn of events, Dick realized that it was actually *fear* that motivated his supervisor; at that crucial moment, the top man sensed he was in danger of losing a good worker who appeared to be craving bigger and better things. So he took the only step that could save the situation—*promote* the assistant.

So, fear became Dick's chief weapon in gaining promotions. First, he would work to prove his mastery of a particular position. This could take as long as two years or more. But at that stage, he would begin to subtly *devalue* his job in the presence of his managers. It was only a matter of time before they became aware of his restlessness, *and their reaction was almost always to move Dick up the ladder!*

This strategy *must* be handled carefully! It helps to know just how far you can go with your boss. Remember, he or she *could* interpret your job-downgrading as simple negativity *if it isn't combined with praise.* You must explain to superiors that your job provides a perfect opportunity *for someone at that level of skill,* but that you have *outgrown* it. (Be sure there are positions you can be advanced to. In a large corporation, this tactic is extremely effective since there are usually many directions in which you can personally expand.)

In only 11 years, Dick advanced to a vice-presidency in the same company for which he toiled as a shipping assistant! Every promotion—and there were many—was prompted by his job-downgrading skill.

In this case, downgrading triggered *fear.* A discussion of that deep human emotion comes later. Right now, it's time for us to talk about the powerful manipulative tactic that works hand in hand with downgrading.

7

The Art of Flattering Your Way to Positions of Big Prestige and Income

Manipulating people to achieve power can sometimes seem to be a game that belongs exclusively to bosses. After all, leaders *already* occupy spots from which they can reach out and use others. *But, you must realize that superiors can be controlled as effectively as employees can!* In fact, when flattery is carefully handled and delicately delivered, it is the quickest way to maneuver bosses! This is true because nearly *all* people—regardless of how much or how little they have accomplished so far in life—are *recognition-starved!* We rarely, if ever, hear words of praise from others, so when we *are* flattered or complimented, we are apt to respond like a starving person jumping on a meal.

It might seem strange to you that an important person (perhaps even the head of a company) could actually be craving for a good word, but it's absolutely true. Most of the individual's employees, family members and friends probably never bother to acknowledge his or her accomplishments, so the door to control of that person through flattery is wide open to the manipulator.

This chapter provides proven flattery strategies which can be used for controlling people and events. It gives you one more awesome weapon for gaining tremendous influence *at once!*

How Kristine W. Conceded Influence to Achieve a Nearly Impossible Goal

Kristine W. found herself in direct competition with another person for the position of office manager in the company she worked for. She was a senior secretary, and her competitor had an accounting and management background. So *he* was clearly the front runner for the job.

The woman realized that she didn't have much of a chance to get the promotion if she merely attempted to outperform the more experienced man. He knew his job, was well respected and had all the necessary credentials for the larger responsibilities. So Kristine knew it would take some high-level manipulation to come out on top. Four department managers would make the decision between the man and her, so Kristine made plans to work on this group.

Kristine noted that her competitor did two things in his dealings with the four managers:

1. He put himself on a level with them and acted as an equal rather than as a subordinate (which he decidedly was).
2. He tended to insulate the four managers from day-to-day activities and decisions. This was done in an effort to save them additional work, and to a certain extent to strengthen his own influence.

The woman planned her attack with the accountant's tactical mistakes in mind, and she immediately set out to exploit them. Kristine reasoned that the department heads might not appreciate having the accountant act as if he were an equal. They were being shielded from things that were happening in the company, and Kristine banked on the possibility that this represented a threat to their feelings of authority.

So, Kristine began to put heat on the accountant this way: She began playing the role of *subordinate* to the four key people. She made *no* pretenses about being on the same level they were, and it made each boss feel *flattered, not threatened,* as the man's approach might have been doing. Secondly, she brought each member of this group in on business decisions *that she could easily have made herself.* This *added* to their sense of involvement and *superiority.* Kristine totally avoided insulating any of the four, as her competitor was in the habit of doing. This extremely subtle form of flattery amounts to *purposely letting* others feel as if *they* possess influence and by doing it long enough to *win your objectives!*

The battle was decisively won by Kristine. By using flattery instead of attempting to compete against nearly impossible odds, she received the promotion she had sought.

The Key to Getting Bosses Under Your Thumb

Thus, by making the top people feel *more* important while her rival was busy trying to build his own power, Kristine won the coveted promotion. She knew when to *build another person's ego* rather than being concerned about her own. The fact is, there is no better way (and very likely no *other* way) to maneuver bosses. Flattery has always been the most rapid route for an employee to take in manipulating higher-ups. It also works in romance, in family situations and in controlling social circumstances.

Yet, as obvious a strategy as flattery is, it is amazingly neglected. Relatively few employees bother to use it in rocketing themselves into better positions. And scarcely anyone utilizes it in achieving victory over adversaries in *other* situations. The reason for this neglect of flattery is that people take too much for granted. They wrongly assume that a boss regularly hears compliments. They conclude that to tell a superior of his skill would be considered corny or trite by that individual since *everyone* is full of praise. They just don't realize that a gracefully delivered compliment can be the sweetest thing a person would want to hear, and that *the impact can make the flatterer very, very big in the recipient's eyes.*

Another possible reason for flattery's lack of use is this: Many people find it difficult to compliment somebody else. They simply can't summon the courage to face another individual and express praise—*even when the ability to do so would improve their positions dramatically!* This chapter is almost sure to cure that reluctance in people.

So, if you have not used the extraordinary power of flattery to help yourself, *now* is the time to start. Or, if the *techniques* of flattery have been a mystery to you, the following pages will make them all very clear to you.

The Secret of Flora L's Astounding Rise to the Executive Suite

With no previous work experience to speak of, Flora took a job as a sales clerk in a retail store. In only 14 months, she was promoted to regional merchandise manager. Just one year later, she was named chief buyer of women's clothing and general merchandise manager. What is truly remarkable about Flora's meteoric climb is that the firm she works for maintains a small, elite management group. Promotion usually takes years, and elevation to the plush offices "on the fourth floor" is considered the ultimate honor in this conservative company. But Flora did it in *two years* from a mere clerk's position!

Was it purely her ability? No. True, Flora is bright and quick to learn, but not appreciably sharper than others in the firm whom she left in the dust. It certainly wasn't her background either. It was simply her uncanny cleverness in flattering the pants off everyone in sight. For example:

1. Flora's first manager was a middle-aged man, a veteran of some 20 years in the retail business. He was rather frustrated since he had never advanced beyond department manager and probably never would.

   Within the first week of her employment, Flora told this man that she felt he was the most knowledgeable individual she ever hoped to encounter in the retail business, and that every morsel of advice he cared to impart would be considered a gem by her. Needless to say, he was captivated by this worship, and made it a point to help protect Flora from the hazards that sometimes plagued beginners in this business.

2. From her first hour of work, the clerk also cultivated each and every store customer who patronized her department. Flora lavished attention on people whenever time permitted.

   It was only a matter of time before customer feedback

began to reach the rarified air of the fourth floor executive suites, then filter down to lower company levels. Soon, Flora's knack for handling people became an example used by various store managers to train their new salespeople. Before six months went by, her name was known in every corner of the store.

3. On those rare occasions when the woman personally came face-to-face with the firm's top executives, she made *every moment and every word count:* "I've heard so much about the way you built up this business from one small store," was the approach Flora used on the company president. This led immediately to an invitation to lunch—and to a friendship not long after that.

   "The inventory control system in this store is absolutely ingenious! Did you really design it?" was the opening Flora used when she first met the merchandise manager. Even she would have been surprised to know that the man's title and office would soon belong to her.

The clerk was astute enough to know that compliments themselves would *not* do the trick. There were certain very effective guidelines which had to be observed *before* a strategy of flattery could work. Let's take a look at them.

Five Rules to Follow in Successfully Buttering People Up

If these five basic rules are used, your flattery is *assured* to bring people under your influence:

1. *Sincerity* is rule number one! It is sufficiently important to deserve additional discussion a little later in this chapter, but we'll take a brief look at it right now.

   Nothing will destroy the manipulator's credibility faster than when he delivers flattery without sincerity. Most adversaries spot that act with ease and turn off instantly. There *are* steps you can take to at least *look sincere* (even if you don't *feel* it), and these comprise the information covered later.

2. *Legitimacy* is every bit as essential to the success of flattery as sincerity is. Here's a definition of legitimacy: The particular attribute you decide to compliment *must be real!* You can't *invent* strengths in people, and you can't make up accomplishments they are not responsible for. So if you can't find *a legitimate basis for flattery,* use some other exploitive strategy!

   When meeting other people for the first time, you can *legitimately* comment about their dress, their punctuality, their favorable personality characteristics, or *any* other things you see at first glance that are outstanding. If your relationship goes on for awhile, you can easily select notable accomplishments to compliment.

   Most people are pretty well aware of what their own personal strengths and weaknesses are. Therefore, if you *try too hard* to find an area to flatter, the person will probably be on to you immediately.

3. *Timing* is an important element in flattery since the tactic is all but worthless unless it's used at *just the right time.*

   The most effective moment for flattery is when bystanders are around to hear the good things you say to your adversary. The presence of an audience heightens the impact of the strategy because the person you are dealing with *is that much more inflated by what you are saying.*

   Good timing is also knowing the moment when *a compliment is not necessarily expected.* Try to stay away from flattering *when it seems like an obvious thing to do*—such as when *everyone* is complimenting your adversary for some worthy deed. It's far better to either wait until the cheers have died down, or better yet, to *anticipate* the rest of the crowd and be the *first* one to flatter the person!

4. *Follow-up* was very well handled by Flora, the retail

clerk. Rather than letting her flattery tactics simply disperse into the wind, she turned them into tangible advantages. In one case, she saw to it that a luncheon invitation resulted.

This effective follow-up was pulled off by Flora with words like these: "I've heard so much about the way you built up this business from one small store . . . I'd really enjoy getting the whole story from you. Maybe we could have lunch together next week."

That approach is difficult for most people to resist since they are offered an opportunity to talk about their favorite subject (*themselves*), to someone who is apparently very interested!

5. *Capitalization* is tying the final knot on the strategy. It consists of turning your flattery efforts into a definite, measurable advantage, which should be a big stride toward victory.

   Once again taking Flora as an example, we know that the clerk used her lunch date with the company president to score some very valuable points. The initial flattery *by itself*, was *not* the conclusion of her tactic. Over sandwiches, the woman asked the boss questions designed to get him to tell the story about his struggle to establish his business on a few borrowed dollars. Flora, of course, sat entranced as the tale unfolded.

   When the saga was finished and Flora looked appropriately awed by his story of drive and perseverance, she explained to him that

   a. She felt honored beyond description to be associated with a man of such remarkable character.
   b. She now felt a sense of loyalty to both him and the firm that she hadn't felt before.
   c. She intended to model her own career after his.

How could such a carefully conceived strategy fail to advance Flora by enormous bounds?

Making Sincerity Pay You Fat Dividends

Without sincerity, Flora's flattery tactics would have fallen flat. While her boss definitely did welcome the chance to display his past undertakings to an impressed young employee, he was also clever enough to realize when he was being snowed. So Flora had to make every element of her strategy as real as possible, just as you will when you first use flattery to gain an objective. Now, it may very well be that *you are genuinely awed* with something your adversary has done or said. If so, sincerity comes automatically. It will show in your eyes, voice and mannerisms. The other person will *know* you are impressed, and your strategy will be successful.

But what if you *don't* really feel it? Then you must *act*, the same way a star performs in front of the lights and cameras! This doesn't require special training or knowledge. It merely takes a certain kind of attitude on your part. Here's what that attitude should be:

> *You must prepare yourself mentally* to admire that certain thing about your adversary which you plan to compliment. *You must get yourself to really believe that the trait or accomplishment is special.* It's done the same way an actor actually *becomes* a villain before he plays the part of that villain. When the cameras stop running, he returns to his real self.

So, even if you do not particularly admire someone you want to manipulate, you must still work on developing the ability to temporarily *forget* your feelings, and regard that individual with admiration. It can be a difficult thing to do, but remember this: If people always displayed their *real* emotions about other men and women who entered their lives, it would be catastrophic! You probably play parts on a daily basis just to get along better with the people around you. *So, by merely cultivating that same skill to a greater degree, you can easily master the art of sincerity!*

How Mort G. Discovered the Best Substitute for Money

As sales manager for a large company which was heavily involved in the recruitment of straight commission salespeople,

Mort had to perfect methods for obtaining the services of capable men and women. The tricky part of his job is that he accomplishes the goal without making even the tiniest cash commitment.

When he first started in this position, Mort's tendency was to speak to job candidates in terms of their "future" with the company. He spoke of actual cases where sales representatives performed well and attained high salaried posts in the firm. During each interview, he ran down a list of employee benefits, described frequent contests, and covered the usual fringe advantages. From where Mort sat, the spiel sounded good. But it wasn't getting recruits, and he was bewildered at the lack of response. He couldn't talk about money (at least outside of making a few strong points about *potential* earnings when commissions started to come in). So what else *could* he sell to an individual besides a future?

As a last resort, Mort decided to play down his traditonal pitch, and try some intensive ego-building on his would-be sales people. He reasoned this way:

> If most of the men and women he interviewed *lacked basic confidence in themselves,* what possible good could it do to try to sell them a future as he had been doing?
>
> *Secondly, Mort felt that ego-building was the only way he could make up for his inability to offer salaries or draws.* He was losing as many recruits to lack of confidence as he was to the company's commission policy, and a strategy of flattery seemed to offer him an excellent way to get around both of these problems.

He tried it during his next interview. The person had experienced a string of failures in sales jobs and couldn't care less about the same old story about all the good things that *could* be down the road. Besides, Mort was sure that this individual regarded *every* commision deal the same way; one was just like the other in the candidate's eyes. So Mort laid on the flattery. He told the applicant that his background was outstanding (despite the fact it was devoid of significant accomplishment), and that his appearance and poise would be distinct assets (more than a little true). In fact, Mort based the *entire interview* on building up this person, *not* on extolling the virtues of the company as *had* been his practice.

The results were strikingly different this time. The job seeker, probably for the first time in his entire career, *felt truly wanted. He also felt there were definite reasons why this particular job matched him as an individual!* Issues such as future and income potential are secondary to the applicant's *personal optimism.*

Flattery became Mort's chief recruitment weapon from that point on. To him, it's as strong a selling tool as offering big salaries.

A Management Trick Every Manipulator Has to Know

So far, we've concentrated mainly on the use of flattery in one-on-one situations. But what about the manager who has a *number* of people to control? He or she is faced with applying flattery (and other exploitive strategies) on a mass basis.

Since flattery seems to be a highly *personal* way to control others, it wouldn't *appear* to be adaptable to group situations. After all, we carefully select the strengths and accomplishments of our adversary, then compliment our way to a position of supremacy over that person. The vital question is, *does a group possess anything personal enough to flatter?* Yes, it definitely does!

Any assembly of people, whether it is within a company or social organization, has three characteristics:

1. *A Personality*
   In any body of people, the sum total of all the individuals' personalities creates a definite *group* personality.

2. *A Level of Proficiency*
   Just as the group has a personality, it also takes on a certain *skill level.*

3. *A Pride Factor*
   The attitude of every member results in a group feeling

of self-respect. It's actually a sensitivity about how outsiders view the work they're doing.

A capable manager will know where his or her group stands *in all three* of the above areas. Instead of trying to constantly contend with *individuals* (which could easily consume every bit of the manager's available time and energy), the head person can exert control *by manipulating the group.*

The very best way to handle a number of people is through that classic institution known as the business meeting. In a meeting environment, the total *group personality* can easily be sensed by the manager, and the total *group pride* is extremely vulnerable. Therefore, flattery in this situation can be enormously powerful.

The juiciest benefits to be gained by manipulating groups through flattery lie in the field of sales management. But the strategy applies in virtually *every* set of circumstances where there's a chief overseeing a general corps. Let's take a careful look at an example of how one highly successful manager controls the people in his department on a wholesale basis.

Matt W's Plan for Getting the Last Drop of Work out of People

Matt owns and operates a messenger service in a large city. Profitability depends primarily on his 18 drivers making the maximum number of pick-ups and deliveries every working day.

When he first formed the company, Matt established a close relationship with each employee. He was a good manager, so he felt that tight control could best be effected on a one-to-one basis between himself and every driver. He was as wrong as he could possibly be. Matt found himself spending most of his time just trying to keep his people motivated, rather than dividing his time equally between personnel problems and administrative matters, as he *should* have been doing.

What he needed was a method for exerting *group* control. Through his efforts at individual management, Matt had at least succeeded in creating group pride; his drivers were extremely conscious of the company's welfare. But, unfortunately, that wasn't enough to keep them out there working at optimum speed and efficiency.

So Matt decided to try a little group manipulation. He would use the group's pride factor to *make every individual perform.* This was his strategy:

1. Using a weekly company-wide meeting as his platform, Matt would spend a few minutes reenforcing the group pride factor. This could easily be done with simple flattery. He could do this by telling his drivers that they were the best in the business or by letting them know that the prior week was profitable because of their efforts.
2. Having successfully achieved a significant build-up in the collective spirit of his people, Matt proceeded to use this powerful group control tactic:

   He explained to his employees that *any slowdown on the part of just one employee would reflect on the efforts of all the rest!* In other words, a slipping in a single individual's performance could have a detrimental effect on the pride every driver was working so hard to protect.

While no one driver would ever privately admit to being influenced by such a subtle threat, Matt knew very well that *no* person in his employment would be likely to take the chance of losing the good will of the others by damaging the group pride! The greater the pride Matt was able to build, the more heavily he was able to assert his threat. The owner had found one of the most successful strategies known for handling large numbers of employees. The proof was in the results: Matt's gross dollar volume leaped over 20 percent almost from the same moment he started using a combination of flattery and threats in his weekly meetings!

Seizing Influence Through the Grapevine

The "grapevine" is very real. It exists in government, in companies, in social organizations and in families. It's an undefinable network of people that is most efficient in passing information along almost as quickly as a telephone can do it.

You may be part of a grapevine right now without realizing it. If you have ever heard a story (true or not) from one person and related it to somebody else, you did your share in creating a grapevine situation. When this phenomenon is used to carry messages of gloom, it's called a rumor mill. But we're going to see how the unseen information network can be used by you to amass power and control, *not* rumors.

So far we've covered the strategy of flattery as applied *directly* to individuals and groups. Now we'll see just how *subtly* flattery can be utilized when it is *indirectly* applied through the grapevine. First, read this rule—and always keep it in the back of your mind:

> *When you find yourself part of a large number of people, and you say something about a particular individual to another person in the group, you can be 90 percent sure that the thing you said will rapidly get back to the person you said it about!* And don't forget this: Flattery travels along the network almost as rapidly as gossip does!

So, for heaven's sake, why not use flattery in the grapevine? It is *especially* helpful if you're a little nervous about buttering people up in face-to-face situations! Can you imagine anything more impressive happening than when the president of a company hears from his secretary that a lower level employee idolizes him? The top men and women are accustomed to hearing *non-productive gossip* through the grapevine, *not* compliments!

Who you tell doesn't matter very much. But to be sure that your flattery gets off to a good start in its journey toward the correct person, tell *more than one person.* Also, select your ultimate target carefully. Make it someone who can do you some good; *when the grapevine has done its job, that person will be a strong ally of yours.*

Be patient! Although the network usually carries your remarks with amazing speed, it *can* sometimes take time for your words to reach the target.

A purchasing agent for a large corporation used flattery in the grapevine to gain some very impressive goals. This is how she did it.

Roberta T's Subtle Climb to Power

If there was ever an instance where an enormously successful strategy was stumbled upon purely by accident, this is it. Roberta T. was painfully shy. Although she definitely wanted to rise to higher positions and earnings, she could never bring herself to attempt taking control over another person, much less use flattery in a personal confrontation.

This woman was a purchasing agent for a major aerospace manufacturing plant (she is now director of purchasing for that firm). Because of her extreme shyness, Roberta was able to cultivate only a small group of friends. She confided in these three people, but rarely spoke at length to others unless it was necessary in conducting business.

Roberta admired a group vice-president who had an office not far from her working area. The executive was, she felt, a strong, yet considerate leader who apparently had earned the respect of everyone he came into contact with. One day, in the course of normal conversation, Roberta expressed her esteem for this man to one of her friends, and never imagined what the result would be.

The grapevine took her observation to the vice-president's ears in a matter of two days. The man was delighted at this positive feedback and made it a point to tell Roberta about it. She then realized the potential of the mysterious network that carried information so quickly.

Rather than being upset that one of her friends had evidently repeated her confidential compliment to somebody else, Roberta decided to take a constructive approach and use her comrades as a kind of outlet to influential higher-ups in the company. Her first step was to map out a specific strategy, which included those *people in the firm who could get promotions for her.* Once these individuals were identified, she concentrated on the *sort of praise she could feed into the network that would serve to direct their attention to her.*

Roberta set about the task of listing four well-placed executives. She also included details in her plan about what these people were accomplishing, a few personal attributes she had observed, and various other facts she had gathered about them.

For a person so shy in one-on-one relationships, the purchasing agent had embarked on a remarkably aggressive campaign for personal advancement! Yet, she was totally comfortable with it since everything, hopefully, would be done *automatically* through the grapevine she had discovered by accident!

The compliments were planted gradually, over a period of several months. Just past the four-month mark, things began to happen. The first sign that her indirect flattery was reaching the proper targets was an important special assignment that came to Roberta from higher up in the organization. Following that, there was a series of other events that indicated she was being seriously considered for bigger things. Then, finally, the promotions came that eventually led to her director of purchasing title.

Roberta T. proved that manipulating people to achieve personal objectives does *not* have to be done through confrontations. She accomplished it beautifully through imaginative use of the grapevine!

The "Trojan Horse" Method of Winning Showdowns

Homer's *Iliad* describes how Greek warriors, unable to scale the high Trojan walls after nine years of siege, built a huge wooden horse and left it outside the enemy gates. The Trojans, thinking the Greeks had finally departed and convinced that the horse was a gift, opened the gates and pulled the horse into the city. Greek soldiers hidden inside of the gigantic wooden structure waited until nightfall and then stormed the city to eventually secure victory.

The strategy was brilliant in two ways: 1) It achieved total surprise, and 2) it utilized *flattery* (which a gift most definitely is). *You can use a wooden horse strategy of your own to overcome tough adversaries.* Here are the circumstances where it works best, and how to do it.

When you are faced with overcoming extremely difficult

opposition under "showdown" conditions, the Trojan Horse strategy is very likely your best choice. For example, let's say you're an investment expert, and you have scheduled a sales presentation before the Board of Directors of a large company. If you successfully close the deal, it will mean a huge commission for you, and a substantial profit for the firm you represent. But one or maybe two of the people you will be addressing are resisting an investment program.

In this case, when planning your Trojan Horse strategy, it's important to know why certain people oppose you, *but it is of paramount importance to have knowledge of what kind of people your opponents are.* You *must* know what their major accomplishments have been in the recent past (this information is usually easy to come by since the individuals themselves try to publicize their good deeds).

Now you are ready to move. First, you present your investment program at the meeting. Then, instead of asking for an affirmative decision from the board as you would normally do, *you go to work on the people who you expect trouble from—the ones you have found out about.* It's done this way: As soon as you have finished your presentation, you thank the panel for the opportunity to present your investment plan. Then, *before anyone has a chance to intervene*, you tell the group that you are especially honored to work with Mr. Adams, Mrs. Smith, or whoever else you feel is a potential enemy. You spend a moment talking about the *specific details* of each adversary's recent heroics and do anything else you can to glorify these individuals before the others present.

Then, and *only* then, do you ask for an OK to draw up the contract. True, your dissenters may *still* vote against your plan, but at least *you have taken the strongest action possible to gain their support!*

With such a strategy, you have done the following important things:

1. *You achieved surprise* just as the Greeks did with their colossal horse. Instead of waging a running battle with

your antagonists, you managed to get behind their defenses swiftly, quietly and unexpectedly.

2. *You utilized the power of flattery.* You presented the wonderful gift of praise at a time *when it meant the most,* when the recipient's peers were present and listening!

It *does* take a little raw nerve to compliment big people in the presence of other big people, but the potential winnings are well worth any temporary discomfort you may undergo!

The Conquest of a Corporation: How Cal V. Changed the Rules

As the only non-technical employee in a high technology company, Cal V. found himself in a position where he either *had* to get control of others, or else accept a position devoid of authority. He was a general manager in a firm composed entirely of mechanical engineers.

Every Monday morning at 8:00 a.m., management meetings are held in Cal's company. He and eight other department heads (all technically oriented) sit down with the firm's president and discuss how things are progressing, problems that may have come up and so forth. Cal discovered that these meetings had deeper implications than they appeared to have at first glance. They were, he learned, *an arena where personal status was achieved or lost.* At these three to four hour sessions, the importance of certain people and jobs were either enhanced or devalued.

At first, this alarmed Cal. What chance did he have to advance the standing of his job and the jobs of the people in his department as the firm's only non-technical manager? The others would almost certainly join forces against him in crucial issues. Even the company president leaned strongly toward technical matters. Cal knew he had a battle on his hands, and he intended to win it.

The first step was to establish the importance of his department in no uncertain terms. Starting one Monday afternoon, Cal embarked on a small-scale public relations program within the company. During that week, he made sure that every other department head knew what he was personally contributing to the business's success, and who his people were and what *they* were doing. The main thrust of his message was: *My staff helps this firm prosper. It does not take a back seat to other departments just because it's personnel are not engineers!* This set the stage for Cal's strategy, as you will see in a moment.

By itself, this rather firm stand would almost surely create resentment among the technical people, and Cal knew it. So he *combined it with flattery directed at the other managers.* And he timed his praise to get the greatest possible impact. As you have probably guessed, the impact Cal needed was available at the Monday meeting. All during the preceding week, the other managers (*and* the company president) had been hearing about the good Cal's staff was doing, and they were ready for more of the same propaganda as they took their places around the conference table. But Cal surprised them.

At this particular meeting, the manager targeted on two of the technical managers he sensed would be especially difficult to deal with. During the meeting, Cal mentioned to the entire group that these two managers—and people in their departments—*had provided particularly valuable assistance* to him and his people in working on several projects.

This was the *last* thing the managers expected to hear from Cal, so it caught them completely off balance (the effect of his praise was magnified *because of the build-up Cal had been giving his own department during the week!*) If not outright supporters of Cal's staff, at least the two people he had complimented became silent friends of his!

As time went on, this clever manager gained even more status through strategic flattery. In only several months, his department was regarded by everyone in the company as equal in influence to any of the coveted technical sections.

For the man or woman who uses manipulative tactics in gaining advancement, increased authority and prestige, flattery is a weapon that is utilized on a daily basis. One other such tactic, used less frequently because of its immense force, is *fear.* Since it is actually a perfect opposite of flattery, this is an excellent time for us to see how it works—and how it can work for *you.*

8

Controlling Others Through the Enormous Power of Fear

Sometimes "nice folks" *do* win. Occasionally, gentle good-natured men and women reach positions of prestige and influence in business and in other aspects of their lives. Some eventually get to the upper echelons of government, and a few operate their own businesses. *But it is the exception rather than the rule.* This rare breed of human being somehow manages to achieve success by appealing to the "reasonableness" of others. The failure rate in this sort of trusting approach is, unfortunately, too high to be practical for most people.

The odds are strictly in favor of the tough leader who knows how to use fear and other exploitive tactics in controlling people and events. This individual is the one you'll find in leadership roles. He or she controls most of the wealth, and receives the major share of respect. The fear-wielding manipulator does *not* naively rely on the good faith of others; he or she believes *only* in the fact that proven people-handling strategies *work*. They get the desired results time after time, almost without fail.

In this chapter, we'll closely examine fear, one of the leading manipulative tactics—yet one of the most sparingly used because of its deep emotional impact. By merely understanding how this dynamite works, you can be virtually immune to its forces, and thus safe from being used by others. On the other hand, to be *adept* in the wielding of fear is to be on the very threshold of breathtaking personal achievement *without being at the mercy of the people in your life who invariably want things their way.*

How Dave Y. Discovered Fear-Power

Dave had been a maintenance worker at an industrial plant for 10 years. He had originally applied for the position with only a basic knowledge of machinery and enough common sense to keep things running in a factory. But the company owner had given him a chance, even with his scant experience in maintenance. Dave was completely satisfied with his modest salary. It was enough to provide a satisfactory existence, and many semi-skilled people Dave knew hadn't done nearly as well.

As the years passed, the plant continually updated its manufacturing techniques and procedures. New equipment was purchased and the factory's production capacity doubled. It grew from a small business to one of the most important in the industry. During this time, Dave received on-the-job training in the care of the sophisticated new machines. His salary increased $2,500 a year after five years with the firm.

The maintenance man became increasingly proficient; by merely listening to machines, he could diagnose and deal with problems before they became serious. Within a few more years, he knew almost as much about the machines as the field representatives of the companies that made them.

On his tenth anniversary with the firm, a party was given for Dave. At the festivities, a company vice-president announced that through the guest of honor's skills, the firm had the industry's lowest machinery down-time, which saved some $100,000 in production that would have been lost. Dave was informed that his salary was to be increased another $2,500.

Most people would have been elated with the raise, but Dave realized that with the exception of the company owner and one secretary, he was the firm's senior employee. It occurred to him that, notwithstanding his contribution and loyalty to the company, *his salary level was still far below that of junior executives fresh out of college.* While he deeply appreciated much that had been done for him during his 10 years with the organization, *he now saw just how little it really was.*

The next day, Dave wrote to a competitive firm. In the letter, he described his mechanical expertise and his excellent job record. To be safe, he did *not* identify his employer. He wrote that he might be interested in a position consulting with the company's clients; seeing that their equipment was installed and running properly, utilized to optimum capability and so forth. Dave was aware that a number of machine producers had chronic service problems. A few days later, an official of the competitive firm replied to the letter. The man offered Dave precisely the job he had inquired about, at a salary of $25,000 a year. Dave said he'd let him know.

The next morning, Dave met with his boss. As soon as he sat down, he thanked the executive for his generosity through the years, *then politely resigned!* His boss came as close to falling out of his chair as Dave had ever seen; the owner literally turned white. In his shock, the company owner managed to ask Dave why he wanted to leave the firm. Dave replied that he felt the top had been reached in his present job. He concluded by offering to remain on his job long enough to train someone else in *the intricate and complex workings of the valuable machinery in the plant.*

Before the end of the day, Dave was summoned by the president. The boss offered him a huge salary jump, an assistant, and participation in company management benefits. Dave accepted.

Although discovered quite by accident, *fear* had totally changed the direction of his career in a matter of hours. *By grasping the most prominent vulnerability in his employer* (an obsessive concern for the expensive machines in the plant), *Dave had achieved his fondest goals!*

You Can Score Stunning Personal Advances by Attacking the Insecurities of Other People

It's safe to assume that Dave's boss spent hours fretting about what would happen to his expensive machinery if his experienced maintenance man left the firm. You can be sure that the president vividly imagined a beginner trying to do the job, botching it and eventually losing most of the big money Dave had saved in reduced down-time over the years.

This company head, despite his sophistication in business

matters, was attacked (however accidently) where he was woefully weak. He might have been a brilliant engineer and a superlative financial planner, *but he was extremely insecure about the upkeep of his machines*—and *that* is how Dave reached him.

The owner of a highly profitable mail order firm is tough about every aspect of his business except *secrecy*. The thought of someone getting their hands on his mailing lists drives the man to sleeplessness.

An otherwise adept bank teller goes to the brink of absolute panic if somebody gives her reason to believe her job is in jeopardy. Because of this, she is highly susceptible to exploitation by her supervisor—who *sees* the woman's fear and knows how to use it to his advantage.

Insecurities exist at *all* levels, and wherever such a personal weakness exists, it's an ideal target for manipulation by fear. *But, the average person doesn't realize how much striking power could be theirs by using fear against these insecurities.* That's why the tactic is *not* used more often *and why most people never rise above low levels of achievement.*

Again, most of the people who have reached positions of prestige and wealth *know how to recognize fear* and *understand how to use it when they see it.* These strong individuals are *not* prone to sympathize with women or men who are insecure. Now, this *doesn't* mean that you go around wearing a scowl, searching for people who display fear about certain things. It *does* mean that in the normal course of your daily business or social activities, you will know how to spot *a fear vulnerability* and do something about it if such a tactic can help you attain your goals without doing harm to another person.

Let's cover a set of guidelines that will give you the fundamentals of putting together your own fear strategy.

Darryl V's Six Rules for Perfecting Razor-Edged Fear Skill

Darryl V. is a young attorney. Just about two years after he passed his bar exam, he was earning almost as much as well-established lawyers. He had reached success while many of his contemporaries were still struggling to get a foot in the door. Darryl attributes his rapid climb to *a knowledge of the workings of fear.*

"I have found that fear works against opposing lawyers, with witnesses, clients, and sometimes even with entire juries," Darryl says. "Any professional person who *doesn't* use it is attempting to operate at a severe disadvantage." He describes the guidelines he established to build his considerable fear-skill:

1. *Get Rid of Misguided Sympathy for Others*

   Darryl feels that when victory is on the line—and within reach—it's no time to let your compassion for the adversary stop you from achieving your goal. He relates an example:

   A key witness has information that might clear Darryl's client. The woman is highly nervous, and would suffer embarrassment if compelled to divulge these facts before a jury. It would be much more comfortable if the lawyer could spare this vulnerable witness a painful ordeal, but *a favorable outcome for Darryl's client is all that matters.* So, he doesn't hestitate to proceed with a tough cross examination which gets the job done in getting the real story out.

   In *your* case, do *not let sensitivity for other people keep you from getting control.* As long as your adversary's discomfort is temporary—and in no way damaging to that person—*you must go ahead with your strategy!*

2. *Learn to Spot Fears in Your Adversary*

   You can't very well use a fear strategy unless you have first identified a fear weakness in the other person. Darryl explains that many people reveal their greatest anxieties *by spending an unusual amount of time talking about them.* The attorney describes this phenomenon:

   "It's strange, but most clients who attempt to conceal certain fears actually go into tremendous detail about those fears during our conversations! Since a particular fear is quite naturally magnified in the person's mind, I guess they can hardly help but talk about it, even though they may think they are covering it up. So my secret is to *listen*, and listen carefully. By the end of most one-hour interviews, I *know* what the person is afraid of!"

3. *Determine Whether the Fear in That Person is Usable*

"The fear factor must be adaptable for use in a strategy before you can exploit it to get that individual under your control," explained the lawyer. He provided this illustration:

"If your adversary is terrified of mice, you can't very well open a box of them during negotiations. But if you *know* that the person is deeply afraid of testifying before a courtroom full of people, you can easily use that as a wedge to get your way."

4. *Ascertain the Best Time to Use Your Edge Over the Other Person*

Flattery is most effective when done in front of other people. But fear, says Darryl, is best used on a one-to-one basis. Whenever possible, the lawyer does his manipulating outside of the courtroom, almost always *before* a trial or hearing starts. The reason is that very often well-meaning people who witness a fear strategy taking place will jump in and *reassure your adversary*. Of course, this can't happen if it's just you and one other person.

5. *Know How to Make Your Tactic Pay Off*

There is absolutely no advantage to finding a person's fear weakness, then using his vulnerability for no specific purpose. *You must have a plan worked out, whereby you'll reap benefits as a direct result of your fear tactic.* Darryl frequently uses his leverage as a means of gaining information and/or cooperation. After he locates a fear weakness in a person, he utilizes *threats* to get his way (more about the power of threats later in this chapter). *Repeat:* You must be ready to *demand personal advantages* the moment you successfully exploit fear!

6. *Fix Things Between You and Your Adversary*

If the fear tactic you use causes the other person

discomfort, as it almost always will do, you can't leave things that way. Darryl gives us the main reason why:

"Most reactions to threats are strong, but short term. In other words, your adversary might be frightened by your threat, but this fright will wear off—sometimes rather rapidly. So, you have to take your advantage fast, *then quickly return your relationship to normal.*

"By making things OK between yourself and your adversary, you are guaranteeing that whatever advantages you gained will remain safe. But, if the relationship is strained, the other person is much more likely to become upset at having been exploited by you, and might decide to go back on whatever agreement was made as soon as the full impact of what you did hits home.

"Usually, all it takes to normalize the relationship are gestures of friendship and consideration from you. Let the person know that you have respect for him or her, and that you really value the friendship. Most intelligent people realize that business is business and what you did was nothing personal."

Those are the basic steps used by a man who is truly an expert in the use of fear. One of his most effective methods for instilling fear in people is now revealed to you.

The Remarkable Strategy of Taking Away What Was Never There

Earlier, we talked about creating illusions to make people believe what we *want* them to believe. The following fear tactic, used extensively by our attorney friend, is also based on setting up an illusion.

Darryl devised an ingenious system whereby he could *manufacture something the other person would be in danger of losing.* You read right! Darryl simply *creates* an illusion for his adversary, then in the next breath, *threatens to take it away* unless he receives what he's asking for! This tactic almost *never* upsets the other individual since there is very little emotional involvement. You can imagine that fear of losing, say, a personal possession or privilege could very well push a person to desperation. But fear of losing something *they don't actually own* doesn't carry the same implications, yet it gets the job done just about as efficiently! Here are examples of how it works:

1. Occasionally, Darryl detects anxiety on the part of witnesses regarding the length of time a trial might take. Using this very real fear factor, *he creates an illusion* of a lengthy trial (by describing how some proceedings drag on for many months). He then promises to do everything he can to get quick proceedings *if he receives all the information he's after!* It works.
2. When the lawyer interviews certain clients, he senses that he isn't getting accurate or complete facts. Needless to say, *by painting a word picture of freedom as opposed to the possible penalties that could result from losing the trial,* he gets complete cooperation.

Success of this remarkable strategy requires two things of you: (1) The ability to spot a fear factor in the other person, and (2) skill at guessing what would be important to that person (usually something they don't presently have, but would *like* to have). Finally, you merely have to threaten the loss of that illusionary "something."

You have probably gathered by now that threats are part and parcel of fear. It's time to see just how closely related they actually are.

Joe L.: A $1.5 Million Fortune Through the Art of Threats

In most job interviews, the applicant stands the best possible chance of being chosen for the position if he or she has no apparent background or character weaknesses. But when Joe L. selects people to work as employees in his company, it doesn't work that way.

Joe operates a highly successful importing firm. He understands the technical workings of his industry well enough, *and he knows what makes people tick.* His one major problem is that he'd much rather remain isolated from his people than deal with them. But, the business has prospered *despite* Joe's hermit-like tendencies, because *he hires people he can dominate by remote control*—through *threats.*

The first step in this extraordinary system is that contrary to common practice, Joe searches applicants for vulnerabilities that center on fear. The importer specifically looks for these key characteristics during the interview:

1. *Tenseness* on the part of the applicant. Joe knows he's on the right track when a job seeker displays nervousness. It tells him that the person can probably be shaken rather easily if required.

2. *Insecurity* goes a bit further than tenseness and is also a welcome characteristic in Joe's opinion. It indicates a basic lack of confidence in the person, even though he or she can demonstrate adequate skills in whatever job is in question. Joe knows he can use threats to successfully control an insecure employee.

3. *Subservience* doesn't necessarily come from lack of confidence, but it gives Joe a very strong grip on an individual just the same. Subservient employees are powerfully "boss-oriented"; right or wrong, they'll follow the leader and jump when he says "jump."

So, *every one* of the importer's 63 employees—at all levels of responsibility in the company—fall into one or more of the above three categories. By the owner's design, it is an extremely threat-prone group. While Joe's firm is definitely not the happiest place in terms of personnel morale, *it is tightly run—with a minimum of direct supervision.*

Although you may have occasion to operate on a somewhat smaller scale than Joe L. does, this strategy is still perfectly sound. People who happen to be afflicted with sensitivity to fear but are otherwise skillful workers are *super-vulnerable to being controlled by threats.*

Getting the Maximum Impact out of Threats

The basic secret to Joe's success in manipulating his help through threats is this: *He establishes definite performance parameters for every employee, and if anyone steps outside of these bounds, Joe lets them know they are in jeopardy.* The fact is, threats become effective in controlling people *only* when parameters like this exist. For example, if you are a restaurant manager and you want to tightly control your waitresses and waiters, you *first* let them know exactly what your rules are and what you expect from them in terms of work performance.

Then, the moment you detect a violation of your rules—or a failure to produce—you can come down on the guilty party as hard as you want—with *full justification.* Even Joe L., with all his skill in using people, could not get away with making up rules as the game progressed. Normal men and women (*including* those who are extra fear-sensitive) simply will not tolerate being threatened *unless they know in advance how they are supposed to act.*

So, as a manipulator, you have to spend some time setting up behavior guidelines that your people *must adhere to.* Here's a suggested procedure for establishing parameters that should go a long way toward making you adept in the use of threats:

1. *Determine what you want to accomplish.* Make a realistic estimate of what you can expect from a person, then figure out what your goals are. Somewhere between the two lie your expectations. Here's a case in point:

   If you are a campaign manager and victory for your candidate in the election depends on your workers covering every neighborhood at least once a week, *that's* a goal. On the other hand, you know that most workers hold regular jobs, and a heavy weekly load might be a tough schedule to meet, so you adjust your expectation as follows: It's reasonable for each worker to cover every neighborhood once every 10 working days. *That* becomes your parameter. It's simply a compromise between what you'd like to have and what you can actually obtain.

2. *Tell every person exactly what the parameters are and what the consequences may be for failing to measure up.* This way, nobody can ever accuse you of being unjust, biased or grouchy. The rules are set, *and your people know you'll be on them if they fail to deliver.*

3. *Come down hard to give your strategy validity.* Joe L. suffers from no credibility problem because he'll fire people occasionally when his rules are bent. This, of course, makes believers out of those who suspect he's all talk.

   Earlier, we discussed the use of manipulative tactics in mass applications. Threats, too, can be used on huge audiences. Here's how.

The Secret of Mass-Scale Fear Manipulation: A Revealing Profile

This amazingly potent strategy is used with profound effect in the field of advertising, but it can also be readily adapted to virtually any situation where you want to gain supremacy over comparatively small groups.

It's quite easy to identify major fears that thousands, even millions of people have in common: Middle-aged people sometimes go through periods of career anxiety; young women and men worry about how they'll make it in the world and so forth. Mass-scale fear manipulation is based on such group problems.

Here's a brief case history that illustrates how an enterprising person used the mass-fear factor to gain an important personal objective:

Carlos G. assumed a marketing post that put him in charge of increasing the circulation of a monthly magazine which featured various small business opportunities. In the process of investigating ways to boost sales of the publication, he decided that his market consisted primarily of *any person who was currently an employee but wished to own a business.* The trouble was, traditional advertising approaches such as "MAKE MORE MONEY," "BE YOUR OWN BOSS," and other similar pitches, were not getting the kind of heavy subscriptions the marketing man was after.

So, he made up his mind to *directly attack the mass-fear factor* in this huge army of frustrated employees. Since Carlos felt that their fear was centered on *job insecurity,* he was sure it would be extremely effective to *play on that anxiety* rather than talk about more abstract concepts like higher earnings and independence.

The campaign Carlos devised got right to the very heart of insecurity; it came out and *told the prospective magazine subscriber that his or her job could be eliminated in a moment and that applicants past a certain age inevitably encountered bias in hiring practices. He also made a point out of the fact that the economy was not in favor of jobhunters.* His ads concluded, of course, with an invitation to subscribe to the magazine. This approach was bold and abrasive, so it predictably drew criticism. But at the same time, it succeeded in nearly *tripling* the best quarter on record for new subscriptions! The threats of job catastrophe made the opportunities magazine extremely attractive to a huge number of frightened people!

If you are in the position of dealing with a number of people, and the group as a whole can be attached to some sort of fear factor, there's no reason why a tactic like this won't work as well for you as it did for Carlos.

Claudia B's Exploitive "Cold Shoulder"

While we're dealing with the use of threats as a means of control over people (especially insecure people), let's cover one more very good way to go about it. In Claudia's case, supremacy in a relationship is achieved through *absolute silence!* When this successful theatrical agent decides it is time for her to gain the upper hand over another person, she does so with the classic "cold shoulder."

As an agent to show business celebrities, Claudia is very good at the game of building egos through flattery. Her clients are accustomed to being idolized and pampered. They thrive on that kind of treatment. These people get buckets of attention from their fans, their friends, hotel owners and almost everyone else, so Claudia is compelled to join in the softsoap if she is to maintain good relationships with her people. She learned a long time ago that flattery is the best way to control people with hungry egos. But she found that praise did *not* always help her when it was necessary to *dominate* one of her client celebrities. To do this, Claudia turns to the cold shoulder tactic. This simply entails a program of *ignoring the individual for a long enough time to get control.*

Specifically, Claudia makes her cold shoulder work by:

1. *Not* calling her client on a daily basis as she normally does.
2. *Not* inviting the person to various get-togethers and parties which she does regularly under normal circumstances.
3. *Not* enclosing a handwritten note to the person when she forwards checks, contracts or other mail.

Being somewhat more sensitive to rejection than most people, her client has an extreme reaction to this show of indifference by Claudia. Within a week or so, the celebrity would call the agent and ask what was wrong. *Claudia was then in a temporary position of dominance, and could get advantages or concessions that wouldn't be available at other times!*

Fear was at work very strongly. The client would begin to wonder if his or her career was slipping. *Claudia's silence is a powerful form of threat,* especially to someone who craves attention constantly. Remember, the key to making the cold shoulder work as an exploitive strategy is this: You should lavish attention on your adversary under normal circumstances. Then, *the contrast of silence becomes a tremendous force that gets immediate and dramatic results!*

The "Straw Man" Technique: Getting Forceful Commands Across Quietly Through Innuendo

Outright threats may very well be excessively strong for use on especially sensitive adversaries. Claudia's clients.could, as artists, be classified as sensitive. So by using silence, she utilized a potent form of *innuendo.* This is the art of establishing a definite threat *without* coming right out and saying something that could offend the other person.

There's a trick to making a subtle version of threat called innuendo. Here it is:

> You use a "straw man" to substitute for your adversary. A straw man is some third person; it could be a person known by you, but unknown to your adversary. Or perhaps it could even be someone you invent as a matter of convenience. Either way, this third person is used by you as an example. In other words, *the straw man becomes the target of your threat.*

Because the straw man is unknown to your adversary, you can make almost *anything* happen to that substitute without danger of insulting your adversary. Therefore, when you are in the process of talking to a person you want to control, and you wish to deliver a subtle threat to that individual in order to get action, you simply tell a story about your straw man, *and make him or her the victim!*

The circumstances surrounding your straw man must closely resemble the situation of your adversary. This *assures* you that one hour or one day after your conversation, your adversary *will realize who you were really talking about, and the remark, which seemed so harmless to him at the time, suddenly takes on the proportions of a direct threat and strikes home with immense force.* Yet, there is always a doubt in the other person's mind as to whether you were really talking about him—or the unknown third person you *said* you were talking about.

The following story clearly illustrates how the straw man innuendo tactic works for a very clever people-handler.

The Iron Fist in a Velvet Glove: Paula R's Way of Dominating Relationships

As a dietitian, there are several built-in factors that Paula R. deals with in order to do her job:

1. Her clients are often overweight, or suffer health problems. Therefore, each individual has a valid fear that Paula can use to get her way.
2. These people are extra sensitive about their problems, so the dietitian can't use direct threats to exploit the fear and enforce her instructions.

At first, the woman attempted to get cooperation by being polite but firm. She stressed the health benefits of following rigidly established diets, and most of it fell on deaf ears. It was the most frustrating experience Paula had ever been through.

She grew progressively angrier. In a few cases, she directly threatened her patients by telling them what the consequences of poor eating habits could be. This invariably upset people and resulted in relationships that were further strained; people simply did not want to hear about how obese or sick *they* might get to be!

As a last resort, Paula decided to make dire examples of some third parties (straw men) to get the point across to her patients. She could draw freely from former clients whose circumstances closely matched those of her problem patient. And she could always alter the progress of the case, if necessary, for maximum shock value. A little imagination, if it was used to better someone's health, was OK with Paula.

The first time she had occasion to use this form of threat by innuendo, it worked beyond her wildest expectations: Paula was dealing with a seriously overweight man in this instance. He was violating almost every dietary guideline she had prescribed. As casually as she could, during the course of conversations with him, Paula told of a former patient *who reminded her of her current client in both appearance and in terms of their condition.*

Then she stopped talking about her straw man and went on to a different subject.

The man's curiosity *immediately* got the best of him, *and he asked the dietitian what the outcome of that case was.* Now the door was open! She told him a story of how it took a supreme effort to save his life after he gained more weight and got very ill. She went into lurid detail, and it genuinely frightened her stubborn patient into complete cooperation!

The tactical genius of *not talking* after describing your straw man is that it puts your adversary in the positon of *inviting the threat!* This is *far* more effective than going into the story on your own (which might seem fairly obvious to your adversary). Don't forget, you'll usually get an invitation to describe the straw man in detail *if* you tell your adversary how similar he or she is to that unknown third party and *clam up!*

Knowing Exactly When to Strike by Using Jay D's Five Keys to Perfect Timing

Operators of automobile repair businesses are people who *should* thoroughly understand how to deal with their fellow human beings. They encounter their fair share of suspicion, anger, pettiness, and just about every other hard-to-handle mood.

Jay D. has made an enormous success of his repair garage, and only part of the reason for his good fortune is the result of his knowledge of mechanical matters. The primary ingredient, Jay says, lies in his manipulative talents, and the strongest of those talents is his mastery of exploiting fear in the customers he sees on a daily basis.

When people develop problems with their cars, there are several different fear-factors that may be at work. Concern about cost and worry about inconvenience are the most prevalent fears. Which of those two fears a particular customer has becomes apparent to Jay almost immediately. After he pinpoints the fear-factor, he can usually manipulate the customer at will.

The shop owner has developed a five-step strategy that gives him control in nine out of ten cases. It deals with *how threats can best be timed to give him the advantage.* Here is Jay's plan:

1. *Jay will not use threats unless he needs quick domination of the relationship.* If a customer is reasonable, there is absolutely no reason for Jay to desire command of that person. But, if the going gets difficult (as it frequently does in his business), *the boss will act swiftly to take over.*

2. *Threats are worse than useless if a fear-factor is not clearly evident in the other person.* A customer who has plenty of money (and no fears about the cost of repairs—or about having his car laid up for a week, since he has two others), is certainly a poor threat target.

   That person, explains Jay, is the only one who can almost get away with making demands in his shop. But they are few and far between. The average individual definitely *does* have a fear vulnerability. So, Jay tries to find out what it is, *then uses it to get his way* if such a tactic is needed.

   Remember: It is best not to attempt threats unless the person's fear-factor is obvious to you!

3. *When you have a definite need to gain control and you have identified a fear-factor, the next step is to figure out a threat that will work!* For example, one customer asked Jay at least six times if there was any possibility that a badly needed brake job could be done for less money than the $120 Jay estimated.

   Tiring of this—and knowing that this man's fear was the expense—Jay said, "Yes, I can patch it up for around $50. But you'll need $200 in additional work within three weeks, not counting the personal property damage you may do by driving around with these defects!" Jay hit the customer with a threat of much larger costs unless he agreed to the originally quoted terms. He could also have added a straw man story to *really* make it scary!

4. *If some other manipulative strategy has a chance of working just as effectively as fear, Jay prefers the milder tactic.* He is fully aware of the risk in using fear; it can backfire if the adversary is highly sensitive. On many occasions, he can get by with flattery (telling the customer that his or her car is beautifully maintained and should receive the best available upkeep and so forth).
5. *The fear/threat combination is a safer tactic for Jay when he has no need to sustain the relationship with his adversary.* He is more apt to threaten when the customer is from out of town, or from a neighborhood far from the shop. He is reluctant to use the power of threats to get control of his regular customers, even when they give him a hard time.

The next major manipulative strategy we'll look at *is a must* in your arsenal if you expect to get anywhere at all in this life. Unless you fully comprehend the dynamics of *promises,* you'll spend most of your time being a victim to those who *do* understand it!

9

Using Promises to Reach Any Goal You've Ever Dreamed of

This major manipulative strategy is used at least as often as flattery in the process of exploitation, perhaps more. Almost every human being dreams of achieving certain objectives in life, and those dreams make people extremely vulnerable to people-users who utilize promises. Countless *dishonest* promises are made every day, but we are *not* interested in nor will we concern ourselves with that variety. It is utterly foolish to lie, for the reason that *you can easily reach your objectives through promises by remaining absolutely truthful!* You'll learn how this works in the opening pages of this chapter.

As you read the following case histories about how other people successfully use promises to get their way, please remember this: Most people *expect* to be given *something to work for*—a goal or goals they can attain through their efforts. When *you* are the one who supplies the goals those people work toward, *you* are the one who will gain through the use of promises.

Terri V's Stairway to Riches

Terri took over as national marketing manager for a small company that supplies gift-boxed cheeses to food and department stores. The firm was after doubled sales, and Terri surpassed that quota in less than one year. Here's how she did it.

Terri went on a shopping spree and selected 15 gifts ranging in price from $50.00 to $479.00 at suggested retail. The top of the line was a deluxe microwave oven. Next, she had a catalog made up that showed each item and described it in detail. The marketing manager's new catalog was set up on a point system; it enabled the firm's 32 representatives to obtain the items free if certain preestablished sales quotas were met or exceeded during a three-month period. The more business over quota a salesperson got, the higher the dollar value of the gift they could choose.

At the end of the period, *each one* of the 32 people *had gone over their quotas!* The gifts cost the cheese company just over $8,000, *but profits during that period soared to $75,000!*

That wasn't the end of Terri's campaign. She then promised to supply a free company car to every person who was able to maintain a 20% increase in sales over a six-month period, using the three-month contest sales marks as a basis for comparison. Volume zoomed to the top of the charts in her office, and Terri obtained eight new automobiles for the winners. As before, the cost was *easily* absorbed by the whopping profit records!

After devising a new plan, which included overseas vacations, cruises and other spectacular incentives, Terri resigned her position to begin her own consulting firm. She knew she could *multiply her income by setting up programs like these for other companies*. This woman was well on her way to a personal fortune, and she did it by using the simplest possible version of the *promise* to get increased production from salespeople.

How to Promise ANYTHING . . . And Still Be Perfectly Honest

The trick to Terri's phenomenal business is this:

> *She can make the most extravagant promises imaginable, as long as her ultimate profits cover the cost of what she plans to give!*

So what's the sense of her lying—or even exaggerating—to motivate the firm's sales force? As long as those people are willing to bring in the profits that pay for the incentives promised to them, Terri can pledge to give them the richest gifts she wants to give them. The point is, the *salespeople* are the only ones paying for the program!

The only time you or any other manipulator can be accused of making baseless promises is if the incentive is willfully withheld, and to do that is to kill the goose that lays the golden egg. The incentive industry is a giant and is still growing at a breathtaking pace. That incredibly rich business is based *on the same system of "self-fulfilling" promises we are talking about right now!* So, there is no reason in the world why *you* shouldn't use the same dynamite in gaining your own fondest objectives. Since it doesn't cost you a single penny to *make* the promises initially, you *don't* need money to make it work. The need for money comes *later, after other people earn it for you!*

Mel T's Winning Promise Formula

After only four years in the business, Mel has already become one of the most successful mail-order operators in the $60 billion a year industry. He started his enterprise "on a shoestring," and with so little knowledge of its workings that friends of his strongly advised him to get out while the getting was good.

But, Mel was sure that his manipulative instincts would bring him victory despite his lack of experience. The young man was convinced that huge masses of people were seeking certain personal goals and always would. As long as that was the case, Mel felt they could be sold by promises. For example, he had observed these phenomena, to name just a few:

1. There were literally *millions* of men and women looking for easy ways to make extra money.
2. A huge segment of the population was concerned about proper nutrition for themselves and for their children.
3. Leisure time was dramatically increasing for more people, and many of them were deathly afraid of becoming bored. Therefore, products that could be sold through the promise of endless fun would, in Mel's opinion, make lots of money.

While most other mail-order operators were trying to merchandise their wares by offering bargains and by glamorizing their products, Mel devoted himself to composing copy about *how his products would help bring the buyer all of the benefits that person wanted most in life!* This is exactly how he did it:

For the seeker of spare-time income, Mel offered booklets about how to start and run small businesses. His ads promised that the material would *rapidly open the door to huge cash rewards in a matter of days.*

For the people concerned about nutrition, Mel's copy told of new feelings of *well-being, renewed vigor and improved health* when his food supplement tablets were taken regularly.

His line of sporting goods were accompanied not by the usual claims of quality and value, but by descriptions of future hours spent in *fascinating vacation time activities,* as opposed to the boredom so many people feared!

Mel's promise approach overcame his inexperience in no uncertain terms. His rate of orders per thousand mailers sent was far higher than average. The following details explain exactly how you can develop a promise strategy as effective as the mail-order man's.

A Three-Step Method for Making Your Promise-Power Work Every Time

In the process of controlling the events in your daily business and social life, you'll have *far* more impact on people than Mel does in his mail-order business. Remember, he has to make his promise work through the printed page, but you'll be dealing on a one-to-one basis which is *always* more forceful.

But, in handling people individually and on a personal level, there are certain basic rules to observe when manipulating through promises. Here they are:

1. *Find out what is important to your adversary.* The key here is, what does a person consider important? With one individual, it could be simple cash. Another might feel that a week in Hawaii is the most important objective on earth. Yet, a third may be dreaming of a new power lawn mower.

It doesn't pay to guess; there's nothing at all wrong with coming right out and *asking* your adversary what his or her fondest goals are. In fact, it's a *very* good way to get the other person extremely interested and involved in you and your proposition!

2. *When you know what's important, decide on a material thing that is believable to the person, yet one that will completely satisfy the dream.* Knowing the individual's area of greatest interest, you now select a suitable incentive. *Don't forget*—it has to be something that will be comfortably absorbed in whatever additional profits you anticipate. *There is very little wisdom in offering an incentive that will cause you to spend money that wasn't generated by the other person!*

   The selection must, of course, be appropriate in terms of the individual's interest; a fishing fanatic might not be motivated by a color TV set, but an expensive new rod and reel would likely be an exciting incentive for him.

   Finally, the incentive you arrive at should be *believable* to the other person. Oddly enough, a gift that is *too* rich might remain beyond the person's ability to imagine; in other words, the other party must be able to *clearly see himself owning the incentive.*

3. *Make attainment of the promised item reasonable—and provide a definite time frame.* The easier it is for your adversary to achieve your incentive, the greater his or her efforts will be. But at the same time, you want to have your cost covered. So calculate as carefully as possible *the minimum amount of production you need* from that person to make the gift possible, then present the offer.

   Try to give the other person *sufficient time for victory.* A too-short period could be discouraging and might defeat the purpose of your promise strategy. Also, be cautious about granting *too much* time; you want to avoid putting the gift so far in the distance that it loses its interest, or its reality.

A promise strategy can also be used to further your career if you are employed by others. The following section describes the way one man does it.

Clarence D's Simple Plan for Getting Huge Salary Boosts and Fancy Titles

When he applied for his first sales management job, Clarence was reasonably well qualified, but found himself up against 16 other people who wanted the position as badly as he did. It was one of the most frustrating experiences he ever went through, because there was *nothing* he could think of to say that would impress the man conducting the screening. Clarence answered every question, but the interview was flat and uninteresting. He sounded like he was *reading from a script.* When it was over, the young man just *knew* he didn't have a chance at the job, and he was absolutely correct. After he got the bad news, Clarence vowed that he would *never again get lost in the crowd.* Not only that, *he swore that he would wrap up any job he set his mind to get.*

It would take a little time and research to accomplish this ambitious objective. But the plan Clarence eventually developed seemed fool-proof. This is what it looked like.

When he would first set his sights on a sales management job in a particular company, *he found out everything he could about their most prominent competitors.* Clarence memorized the important details about the product lines of these rival firms, their price structures and their methods of doing business. In addition, he became familiar with every available fact on the company he was applying to. Armed with this treasure of information, Clarence was in a position to *promise his way to almost unbelievable job offers!*

When a typical interview first started, Clarence patiently went along with the routine questions about his background, education and so forth. Then, the moment he sensed that the initiative was going in favor of his adversary (the interviewer), *he would blow the lid off the discussion with a statement like this:*

> Pardon me, Mr. Adams, but instead of our spending these valuable few minutes talking about the usual things you cover with ordinary jobhunters, may I suggest that you and I talk about *what I could accomplish for your firm* against competition like Acme, National and Seaway?

The interviewer is invariably flabbergasted at a declaration of such confidence and audacity. First of all, how does this perfect stranger know who the competition is? Secondly, what could he accomplish without knowing the inside workings of this industry?

But Clarence is ready. He has come to the interview *with a market plan firmly established in his mind.* Whether it's right or wrong, *the interviewer can't help but be deeply impressed by the applicant's desire, preparation and guts.* And, whether the plan is right or wrong, the company representative usually *does believe* Clarence can really accomplish the goals embodied in his elaborate marketing strategy. The young man describes how he can increase the company's market share, how he can neutralize the efforts of the rival firms he mentioned earlier and how he can expand distribution if *he* gets the sales management position.

Clarence's promise strategy rarely fails to land him a fat offer. By simply being prepared, through a little homework, he can *easily* beat out a formidable field of highly qualified men and women!

Pledge Modification . . . Or the Art of Getting off the Hook

So, Clarence D. has no trouble bowling over some hard-to-impress interviewers with meticulously planned promises to beat the pants off the competition. So far, so good. But he has to eventually come to grips with the necessity of making good his pledges—or *does* he? The truth is, Clarence can perform *no better* than any other reasonably qualified sales manager once he gets the job. Most ordinary people facing the necessity of living up to such fat promises would cave in under the pressure—or be fired for failing to meet overly optimistic quotas. But not *this* enterprising manipulator!

Clarence has the ability to neatly get off the hook after he gets the position he was after. The promises are *strictly a device to be used for landing higher paying jobs!* If he *can* increase the company's business, fine and well. But his objective—immediately after he occupies the big new office—is to *modify the pledges he made* so he can protect himself. This is how he does it.

As soon as the new sales manager starts his job, he makes it a point to find "serious problems" in his department. These problems usually include inadequately trained salespeople, lack of strong support advertising, a weak expense policy and literally scores of others. Clarence makes a major issue of his fault-finding; he tells his superiors that *it's impossible for him to generate the kind of business he promised unless the difficulties are taken care of!* By the time one deficient area is cleared up, another one begs for attention. This goes on for many months, and his boss keeps the pressure off.

By the time his *own* department is squared away, Clarence has gotten himself involved in *other* parts of the company; he complains about slow shipping of his orders, about poor billing practices, about indifferent customer service and about *every other thing he can poke a hole in!* Every fault Clarence can find buys him more time, and delays the inevitable day of reckoning. When top executives finally *do* get tired of hearing from him about all the company's shortcomings, the sales manager is ready to move on to another opportunity. So he *repeats* his promise strategy to get an even *better paying* position!

When he *gets* the new job, he *repeats* his pledge modification tactics, and he's good for another two or three years. Remember, this man performs to the best of his ability—and as well as most other people could in the same job. He uses promises merely *to sell himself into the most desirable available jobs.*

Using promises for highly effective recruiting is one more area of extreme importance. Let's see how it's done.

The Fantastic Real Estate Recruitment Machine of Paul H.

While a majority of real estate brokers in a large city suffers from a chronic shortage of top-notch salespeople, Paul H. is easily able to "turn the tap" and get as many as he needs. When he first started in the business, Paul noticed that the broker he worked for was doing well in spite of large turnover. His boss ran sales recruitment advertisements on practically a daily basis in the newspaper. These succeeded in attracting a modest flow of licensed agents. In addition to this, the man was willing to pay for the cost of sending inexperienced people to real estate school.

Through that combination, the broker was able to keep a sufficient number of salespeople out working. So *regardless* of turnover, the current group of agents at any given time would manage to come across enough business to keep the boss reasonably prosperous. It appeared to Paul that turnover simply didn't matter as long as *new* people could be attracted to replace the ones who became discouraged and left the field.

This was the way Paul saw it: If a broker was able to recruit a *huge staff* of new agents, notable success would be bound to occur. The coverage alone would assure more listings and home sales than competitors with smaller staffs could get. Then, if *enthusiasm* was at a high level, the turnover might be reduced and the staff would grow even larger. The beauty of it was that no matter how many people were hired, costs would stay under control because of the traditional straight commission basis prevailing in the real estate industry; *he would be free to use valuable resources at virtually no cost.*

Paul obtained his broker's license as quickly as he was legally permitted to. He had experienced moderate success during the initial six months and had saved every penny he could to finance his plan.

The first step was a ten-day trip to a swank Caribbean resort. It wasn't strictly for pleasure. Paul spent almost every day of this vacation taking color movies—35 reels of them—of everything in sight. As soon as he returned home, he worked day and night splicing and editing to create a 20-minute film of an island paradise. The finished product showed golden beaches, private cabanas, the blue ocean and every other imaginable luxury.

The next step was the rental of a local country club dining room. Paul planned to buy cocktails and dinner for 15 prospective real estate agents and their mates. They would hopefully be his starting organization.

Paul then advertised in the help-wanted section of the newspaper. It was no ordinary ad: it described a free get-acquainted dinner, an expenses-paid trip for two and early promotion to management of a real estate branch office. Paul's competitors were still sound asleep and would remain so. In fact, several of their top sales people responded to the ad, and Paul carefully selected and invited the ones he wanted to attend his initial get-together.

The party started with the usual cocktails, casual conversation and a gradual build-up of inspiration, *which rapidly evolved into almost hysterical group enthusiasm.* Dinner was excellent and served the purpose of cementing Paul's relationship with everyone present. After dessert, the new broker took the podium and presented his success program: complete with graphs, charts and income projections. By the end of this phase, *there wasn't a husband or wife present who didn't have secret dreams of the wealth that was certain to come only a few months later.* It had to—*it looked and sounded so easy!*

Paul's film was the clincher. There it was in front of the eager eyes of his audience—in full color—a fabulous trip *every one of them would get free* if they produced a certain dollar level of business for Paul after four months. It didn't stop there. He even showed the group an itinerary that gave them the time of departure, the names of the night spots to be visited by the triumphant travelers and so forth!

From the 11 agents he hired that evening and the following day, Paul's organization grew to 42 people in six months! He holds the country club session twice monthly now—and can't handle the number of aspiring real estate agents who want to join his company. In the course of a year, he has paid for two trips (comfortably absorbed in his profits), has appointed ten branch managers as he promised he would and his turnover rate is the lowest in town.

In the hands of this man, promises are dynamite!

How a Sharp Operator Keeps Treasures Just out of Reach Through Razzle-Dazzle With Figures

The graphs and charts that real estate broker Paul H. uses in his hard-hitting country club recruitment presentations are every bit as effective as his remarkable homemade travelog. They convincingly portray the steps a salesperson must take in order to reach prosperity. A certain number of daily contacts will result in so many prospects, and a predictable number of sales will come from those leads.

Paul is perfectly aware that in the relaxed and strongly positive atmosphere of the country club dining room, *almost nothing he ever says will be challenged.* The group psychology works this way: If anyone present *is* skeptical, they generally keep it to themselves because the assembly as a whole is at such a high level of excitement. Every guest senses that negative comments from the audience would be met with unanimous disapproval by all the others—plus the dissenter's own spouse.

But, Paul doesn't use the potent advantages of mass hysteria to demonstrate "outrageous" projections. He carefully devises *realistic* figures that display the ease with which the average agent can make $40,000 a year or more. His avid listeners are drawn into the magic of his proof gradually. As each set of numbers is given, Paul asks the entire group to *vocally affirm the credibility of what he is saying:* "Is there anyone out there who would question the fact that 20 contacts each day can easily be made?"

Of course nobody questions it! And by agreeing, they set themselves up for the *next* premise Paul will present. The next one gets them involved yet further, and the process continues until every member of the audience is sitting there making $40,000 to $70,000 a year in their imaginations! It's nothing they haven't heard before at least a dozen times, but the conviction and force Paul puts behind the delivery—and the visual impact of his charts—make it not only utterly believable, but an apparent sure thing!

So the free trip doesn't become just an aspiration of hopeful real estate agents, it turns into an accomplished fact, just a matter of arranging a sitter for the kids. And Paul's proposition becomes the best one in town—the only place to work!

How to Inspire an Audience by Building Dreams of Wealth

Exactly what do Paul and other expert manipulators do to spellbind a person or an entire group? Exactly what is said that creates the kind of powerful enthusiasm that leads to success? Here are the answers:

You take *daily* time increments, and daily income amounts, and multiply them by weekly increments of time and money. Then you project an *annual* income figure based on the weekly numbers. For example:

> "You work only five or six hours a day and make only 15 sales calls in that time—and close just one prospect, which any self-respecting salesperson can do—and you'd make a commission of $83. In a five day week, that's $415 and in one year you have $21,580. Right?"

The person or group invariably voices agreement to these perfectly reasonable numbers.

> "Okay, that was just the tip of the iceberg. Now, let's take a look at *repeat* business."

This easily *doubles* the original numbers.

In handling these discussions, you must never introduce such details as travel time, inclement weather, cost of doing business, cancellations, delivery delays or any of the other annoyances that would make your idealized income projection seem difficult to achieve. Also, you should make it a practice to *ask for agreement after giving each set of figures.*

If you detect reluctance to accept a premise along the way to your conclusion, be ready to give your adversary a more conservative set of figures, ones the other person will buy without hesitation. The employer who is limited to working with established salaries which are set at modest levels can also use this kind of razzle-dazzle. In recruiting and hiring, he or she can turn company growth and expansion into an effective manipulative tool, like this:

> "We expect to double the size of this firm soon. When that happens, your position will grow tremendously—and will command a much larger salary. You're making an excellent investment in the future!"

In this example, the interviewer does *not* tie the salary increases to a measurable quantity such as "doubled sales" or "doubled profits." The words used are "doubled *size*," an extremely difficult milestone to identify!

Manipulative talents are vital to the person who achieves success through the efforts of others. But basic recruitment skills are equally necessary. We'll cover those important techniques now.

10

Where to Find People Who Are Eager to Put Their Efforts to Work for You

Nearly any successful person will attest to the fact that their personal wealth and influence are largely the result of the efforts of others. In most cases, these men and women did *not* make it strictly by their own labors. You might even be surprised at how many prosperous individuals have others do just about *everything* for them! It simply isn't very practical to try to conquer the world with your own two hands. There just isn't time enough in each day.

But the major reason for enlisting other people to help you reach your goals is this: *Your efforts must be multiplied if you expect to make substantial gains.* No matter what the nature of your business happens to be, you have to develop the ability to produce carbon copies of yourself! It's the same thing as focusing the sun's rays through a magnifying glass to concentrate the energy into an overwhelmingly powerful force.

An example of this principle is a woman who started free-lance market research work. By her own efforts, she was easily able to reach over $3,000 in gross monthly billings. But, she found that *she had to turn down another $4,000 to $5,000 in monthly business because she couldn't be in two places at once. As soon as she learned to recruit and control other qualified researchers who could handle the extra business for her,* the enterprise reached enormous prosperity.

This chapter will show you precisely how such recruiting is accomplished. It will put you in a perfect position to multiply your own efforts, thus setting the stage for breathtaking personal and business growth!

Capitalizing on the Incredible Moonlighting Craze

There's an enormous reservoir of people in America who are seeking ways to supplement their regular incomes. Nobody knows for sure how many men and women there are in this massive army of opportunity seekers, but it wouldn't be at all surprising if the number turned out to be many millions. This big chunk of our adult population consists of a wide cross section of people. There are retirees, women raising young children, even a large number of managers, small business owners and scores of other classifications.

These people are constantly searching for ways to generate income—either because they are not earning sufficient money at their full-time endeavors, or because they are striving to finance various luxuries that are out of reach to them under normal conditions. *This is the market you want to understand.* These are the people who will boost you to the goals you have your sights on, *when they are used intelligently!*

A number of companies are successfully exploiting this market. These firms recognize the virtually endless profit potential in helping these moonlighters earn money, and they are busily making the most of the situation. But the surface hasn't been scratched; *there are still far more people seeking opportunities than there are companies or individuals to serve them.*

Your personal gold mine as a manipulator might very well lie in the exploitation of this rich market. Here are just two of the many, many possibilities:

1. *If you are in a small business that you own and operate yourself,* moonlighters can easily be attracted and trained as sales representatives eager to expand your operations. They would generally be willing to work on a commission basis and put in even the most inconvenient hours for a chance to make nominal money for themselves *and a fortune for you.*

2. *If your enterprise requires special expertise such as engineering advice, finance assistance, marketing guidance or any other high-level skill,* you can obtain the services of top-qualified people at rates far below those prevailing in industry. It's simply a matter of finding an expert who's willing to spend a little time to make a little extra money.

This story goes into revealing detail about what a small business operator does to keep a flow of highly talented people coming into his firm to help him prosper.

Wayne W's Never-Ending Tide of People-Power: How He Does it

Wayne W. contacts companies that have just had new computer systems installed. His consulting services are extremely valuable to these firms, since they are faced with training management personnel and a multitude of other chores required in such a changeover. This particular consulting operation is one of the busiest and most profitable in the business. Wayne's rates are just low enough to consistently beat his rivals. He manages to do this because *his payroll and other overhead expenses are half that of other consulting firms!*

Most companies in consulting maintain full-time staffs of highly paid specialists who visit clients and fulfill the agreed-upon services. But Wayne didn't want any part of being saddled with a staggering fixed expense like that. The *only* permanent employees in his firm are himself and a secretary/bookkeeper. His payroll is *less than one sixth* of what his average rival lays out each week in salaries!

How does Wayne operate a highly efficient computer consulting operation without maintaining a large staff? Simple! He merely obtains the brains and talent he needs *when he needs them.* The owner gets *precisely* the right men and women for his purposes from the huge roles of retirees, disabled people and any other group that includes highly trained individuals who are not regularly employed. Wayne also makes extensive use of moonlighters who are eager for extra income.

The unemployed people he uses are not only as skillful as folks who *do* work regularly, but they are especially glad to get assignments from Wayne. And being that grateful for part-time work, they are perfectly willing to accept wages less than their training would demand under normal circumstances. The moonlighters also agree to spend their after-hours time at less than prevailing rates of pay. So Wayne has a pool of top-notch employees at bargain basement prices.

The consultant's method of recruitment is amazingly simple. He maintains regular contact with a group of the largest computer companies and asks the personnel directors for the names of retirees. In most cases, this information is freely given, since it benefits those who might otherwise be excluded from the job market because of age. This contact leads to referrals to *other* skilled people. Once the word got around that Wayne was looking for computer specialists, he had more applicants than he could use in a lifetime.

Let's look at the opportunity seekers more carefully. This section shows you how the "make extra money" appeal is most effectively made through newspapers and magazine ads.

An Inside Look at Five Marvelous Shortcuts that Attract a Torrent of New Opportunity Seekers

The nature of your enterprise has *no bearing whatsoever on your overall recruitment strategy.* The basic principles used in attracting people *always remains the same,* no matter what you are involved in. Therefore, whether you are a personnel manager, a door-to-door salesperson, a fund-raiser, a community worker or anything else, the following *basic tactics* still apply!

These are the crucial points that must be covered when you are attempting to obtain the services of an individual in the "opportunity seeker" classification. The points are *proven* as they have worked *time after time* for some of the wealthiest businesses:

1. *Admit to your potential recruit that he or she is fully justified in not being sure.* Many opportunity seekers lack self-confidence when they investigate various money-making activities. Therefore, the potential recruit you talk to (or write to) must be *reassured* before you do anything else. *Use this approach:*

   "It's human nature to have self-doubt. We resist great ideas even when we're *sure* that wonderful new things will happen to us. *My* formula is to get started *immediately*, while I'm at the peak of excitement and enthusiasm. That's the *best* time to start something new. I hope *you* do that, because I know it will work!"

   You have provided comfort by letting the person know that self-doubt is perfectly OK. And, you've told him that *you* have succeeded by jumping right in, head first.

2. *Offer personal support. This does wonders in dispelling self-doubt and skepticism.* In this step, you let the person know that he will enter the enterprise with you at his side.

   "I'm here to help you in every possible way by bringing you new ideas, new products, lowest prices (or any points appropriate to your offer) and to make sure that *you* make the largest possible profits!

   "In my business, there are *no* tricks, no complicated formulas to achieving success. Just follow the plan I show you, and you'll make it easily."

At this stage, the prospective recruit is beginning to feel a little more relaxed, and is very likely *visualizing* himself as your employee or agent. If this visualization is pleasant, you'll win. So this is what you do to *make* it pleasant:

3. *You provide a realistic taste of the fears . . . then a sampling of the ultimate rewards.* You'll use the promise strategy here, but not before you acknowledge the fact that any normal beginner experiences a certain amount of fear upon entering a new venture:

   "It's natural to have a few 'butterflies' at the start. I *still* get them when I meet with bankers, or with my board of directors. But the rewards are fantastic . . . financially *and* socially. You'll make new friends, you'll enjoy the thrill of being important and you'll make more money than you've ever dreamed of!"

The potential recruit will secretly respect you for describing the butterflies that almost every person feels when entering a new situation. It builds credibility, and makes the promise of rewards more believable.

4. *Next, give your prospect good feelings about where your business is headed.* If you can do so honestly, instill confidence with a statement like this:

   "We've just completed the biggest volume year in our history, and *this* year is headed for new records. I urge you to get in *immediately* on these windfall profits."

Under most conditions, this will do it. Just about any legitimate job candidate will agree to join you. But if *more* punch is needed, try this:

5. *Describe the experiences of another successful member of your organization, or relate your own triumphs.* Such testimonial adds tremendously to the weight of your recruitment effort. Try to use a case that resembles your prospect as closely as possible. That way the recruit will relate more easily to the situation.

Remember, in using these five steps for recruiting, the *actual words* you use should be your own. The important thing is, the person must be *assured* and these points definitely accomplish that. But even with plenty of assurance, you may sometimes have to combat skepticism. Here's how one very skillful insurance recruiter gets around negativity.

How Anita K. Sweeps Skeptics off Their Feet Through Spirit Matching

Besides lack of confidence, the other main enemy of the people-user is skepticism. In your search for recruits, you'll encounter scores of prospects who let *suspicion* keep them from making decisions. Perhaps these wary individuals have been "burned" by someone who misrepresented or failed to deliver what was promised. Whatever the reason, the skepticism *must be dealt with* if the person is to be brought into your sphere of influence.

One of the most effective ways to overcome suspicion is used by Anita K. in her activities as a sales recruiter for an insurance company. This is a highly competitive business, and turnover is far above average. Therefore, Anita must *constantly* bring new people into the company to replace the dropouts.

As soon as a job hunter learns that Anita is hiring for insurance sales, that wall of suspicion goes up, and the person becomes virtually unreachable. The reason why this happens is that a great majority of applicants have been pushed into similar positions by high pressure recruiters, and most of the job applicants later regretted succumbing to the enthusiasm. So, Anita decided that it was fruitless to try and hire these skeptics at the time of the first interview. It was inevitably a vicious cycle; *the harder she tried to convince the wary individual, the further that person withdrew into a protective shell.* She was sure the answer was in a kind of reverse psychology approach. This is how it worked:

The moment Anita sensed she was interviewing a skeptic, *she withdrew all enthusiasm and pressure.* She actually became rather aloof. In effect, the recruiter was *matching the spirit displayed by her prospect!* The more remote and withdrawn her adversary became, the more standoffish *she* became. The doubter suddenly realized that the woman was no longer attempting to get a commitment for a position with the insurance firm, and this disturbed the person noticeably. He or she would begin to wonder what caused the dramatic cooling off.

If necessary, Anita ends the interview by saying, "We'll call you if we feel you'd fit the responsibilities we have in mind." Then she dismisses the applicant. This bold spirit-matching strategy increased her successful recruitments by nearly 75 percent. The idea that the insurance company is actually *that selective* about salespeople is simply too much for even the most hardened procrastinators to handle.

Any adept manipulator like Anita understands how important it is to maintain optimum organizational strength. Some of the best sources of excellent people are *your business rivals.*

Luring Top Help Away from Tough Competitors

Why go to the trouble of locating promising beginners and worry about training them when competitive firms have already done all that *for* you? Some of the most prosperous companies agree that it pays handsomely to operate this way. You may not get *all* the good help you need by relying on rivals as a source, but you can certainly take care of a large part of your needs!

Before we get into a discussion of how this is handled, a word of caution is necessary: Luring top people away from competitive firms *can* pose serious problems. If you become known as "a people stealer," it can severely damage your reputation—especially in a tightly knit industry where many people are acquainted and frequently exchange information and gossip. Therefore, this recruiting tactic is advised *only* in businesses where high personnel turnover is chronic, and where there is a minimum of personal ties between rivals. If not handled delicately, you might get involved in a theft war that can *hurt you as badly as it does your adversary!*

As a "people hunter," you can take some comfort in the fact that *a person will not normally quit a job to join you unless he or she is in some way dissatisfied with the other situation* (the one the individual is currently engaged with). If that is the case, a change will benefit the employee, the former employer *and* you.

The most delicate possible way to begin to lure good people away from rival firms is by getting to know those employees. But the *method* of getting acquainted is all-important.

Your first step is to join as many associations, clubs and professional groups as you can. These different groups should be exclusively for the benefit of the people in a particular industry. Following that solid reasoning, Anita K. belongs to several associations that cater *only* to insurance people.

By attending a number of meetings and social functions, you begin to identify the people you'd be interested in having work for you. The next step is to *gradually* feed this target group the kind of information that you know will eventually influence them. The information can include such facts as these:

1. Your enterprise is growing, and you badly need people who have managerial potential.
2. Profits are at record levels, and even your *less* talented salespeople are at top earnings.
3. The working environment in your organization is outstanding.

In the process of getting these points across, it is *extremely important that you present yourself as a capable, agreeable and progressive leader,* the kind of boss any employee would enjoy working for. In time, your target men and women will *ask you* what the chances are of jumping over to your company. So, if the tactic is smoothly handled, *you* are not the one who instigates a change! You are merely the one who *sits back and weighs the offers that will come in from the people you have so skillfully cultivated!*

Arnie W's Formula for Keeping Business Rivals Under Control

As potent as our "people hunting" strategy usually is, it can still lead to problems from time to time.

Arnie W. owns a small direct-to-consumer sales company. The growth of his enterprise is limited *only by the number of good representatives he can put into territories in a five-state area.* Therefore, he is *constantly* recruiting new trainees—and he obtains them in every conceivable way. As far as management positions are concerned, Arnie has always used *experienced* men and women obtained from competitive companies. In this way, he is able to put *ready-made leadership talent into the field.* In one instance, he hired five managers from one rival firm in a six-week period! It created a scandal that shook Arnie's business to its foundation.

First, he received an angry phone call from a district supervisor of that company. A week later, he heard from a trusted friend that his name was the talk of that firm, and the talk wasn't flattering. Arnie became deeply concerned. Somehow, he'd have to find a way to soothe the top people in the other company. An apology was ruled out by Arnie because *it was the same thing as admitting guilt,* and it would bring to an end his source of trained managers. The answer came to him in a flash:

There were always sales people in Arnie's firm who did well enough to survive, but were not really making the most of their territories. If they were replaced, sales would very likely grow. Why couldn't it be arranged for *these people to be "stolen" by the competitive company Arnie had just antagonized?* It was the best way in the world to even the score in Arnie's thinking.

Arnie had two of his most trusted managers subtly tell those certain salespeople that a competitive company was looking for experienced reps. This tidbit of information was dropped casually, in the course of conversation—as was the *name* of the company. In a matter of days, *three people were hired away from Arnie's company by the other organization!* Now the score *was* even, and needless to say, the anger vanished. Everyone was happy again!

Four Free Advertising Techniques that Get Heavy Response to Your Offers

If manipulating top people away from rival firms sounds a bit too rough for you, or if you feel as though that method can satisfy only *part* of your people needs, here are four other recruitment techniques that work, but cost you absolutely *nothing.*

1. *Referrals* are far and away the best, most effective way of keeping new recruits coming. If you are in a sales or service business, ask every customer if they know of someone who is looking for a position—or for extra part-time income (whatever the case may be in your situation).

   Also, ask your current employees or agents if they know of good candidates. You might even offer cash finders' fees for successful referrals.

2. *Postings* on supermarket bulletin boards, on college campuses or anywhere people are likely to see them always succeed in attracting a flow of people who are willing to work.

   In some large cities, you'll occasionally find large apartment complexes that have areas reserved for announcements of interest. Whenever you can find them, *use* such opportunities to get your message across.

A typical bulletin board notice could look like this:

MAKE BIG MONEY
TODAY
IN YOUR SPARE TIME!
Call Mrs. Adams
(000) 000-0000

It hardly matters *what* business you're in. A simple notice like this *will get results!*

3. *Plugs in Ads and Correspondence.* If you spend even a nominal amount of money on advertising a product or service, you can easily get a fortune in free recruitment power.

   Let's say you mail a product catalog direct to 20,000 consumers once every three months. *An ad that promises big extra income for ambitious men and women will get dozens of responses if you run it in each catalog—and in every letter you send to customers!*

   The ad could say:

   > MAKE BIG MONEY NEAR YOUR HOME IN JUST A FEW HOURS A WEEK!
   >
   > If you like the merchandise in this catalog, Ajax Distributors wants to talk to you about becoming a regional distributor.
   >
   > You'll meet new people, gain tremendous prestige as a gift dealer . . . AND YOU'LL MAKE MORE MONEY THAN EVER BEFORE WITH LESS EFFORT!
   >
   > Only a few openings are available, so call this number *TODAY:*
   >
   > Mr. Hansen 000-0000

   Since you're sending the catalog anyway, this method gives you tremendous impact at *no additional cost!*

4. *Local Newspapers.* Many publications, and quite a few larger dailies, will not hesitate to print news items about job opportunities. This is doubly true in view of the chronic employment crisis that is said to exist in heavily populated urban areas.

   An article about money-making opportunities would be considered a public service by most newspapers *as long as the text does not publicize the product or service offered by your firm.* Thus, to satisfy that requirement, the news items should deal *strictly* with the fact that a legitimate income opportunity is available for men and women, and it should include only the *briefest* mention of the nature of your enterprise.

Use a straight-forward approach; simply call every publication in your area, and tell them you'd like their help in getting neighborhood people to work.

Using one or all of these proven recruitment methods will *definitely* get you a flock of people who are willing to roll up their sleeves to help you get rich. But before you can actually put them to work, you have to favorably impress the prospect. Here's how one man does it.

Al E's Super-Impressive People Trap Keeps the Trainees Coming

Al owns a jewelry sales company. He employs around 80 people at any given time, and recruitment of new trainees is a never-ending task. Using the four techniques described earlier, plus a vigorous campaign in paid classified advertising, Al does succeed in getting a good response from job candidates. But getting a sufficient number of men and women to actually *make commitments to begin work* was somewhat more difficult—at least until he developed a hard-hitting interview strategy.

But, before we get into a description of what Al does *now* to convert prospects to salespeople, we'll look at how he proceeded when he *first* started in business. When Al had interviews scheduled, he dressed casually, asked a few basic questions about the person's background, then launched into a 20 minute talk about how good the jewelry business was. It was essentially the same interview used by *most* recruiters, and it was *totally ineffective*.

Using this unimaginative procedure, Al had to conduct 18 interviews to get just one sales trainee. Instead of *him* manipulating the prospect, *he* was the one being used! After one year of that wasted time and effort, he decided to use a system that he was positive would be successful over 50 percent of the time; rather than attempt to deal with job hunters as equals, like he *had* been doing, Al decided to embark on a *program of intimidation!*

The owner felt that unless the job hunter was *in awe of the interviewer,* there was very little incentive for that person to want the position. In other words, the *employer had to hold absolute command and respect* during that half-hour to 40-minute session. Since Al realized that he did *not* possess an overpowering personality, he would have to find some other means of making himself seem formidable.

This is the "people-trap" system the jewelry merchandiser developed to intimidate and ultimately convert his opportunity seekers to commissioned salespeople:

1. On interview days, Al dressed impeccably. He wore a suit and tie, and every detail of his appearance was as perfect as he could get it.
2. His preparation for the interview was planned to the finest detail; Al had worked out a penetrating question pattern designed to reveal virtually *every significant fact about his prospect.*

   Part of this pattern consisted of questions that required the opportunity seeker to *describe how he or she would handle a given customer complaint or situation.* There was *no* possibility of bluffing an answer to a question like that, and the person was obliged to think fast.
3. At the beginning of the interview, Al would ask the other person if he had any objection to him *tape-recording the proceedings.* Almost everyone consented, and this served to tremendously heighten the pressure!
4. At the conclusion of the session, the interviewer thanked the prospect and said he'd decide within a three-day period (even if he was *positive* he wanted the person!)

This highly formal, tension-packed job interview made a deep impression on most candidates. Al was right. From the time he started using this people-trap strategy, his conversions soared to nearly 65 percent! He had confirmed beyond any doubt that *casual, friendly interviews just don't do the job.* But it was a different story for sessions designed to put the adversary in a position where *he is forced to respect and perform for the questioner!*

NOTE: Although a formal interview is more effective for most recruiters, its use does not mean you can eliminate the steps for overcoming self-doubt and skepticism, described earlier in this chapter. In fact, these points are *more* emphatic if you maintain a formal demeanor during interviews.

Getting Optimum Power Out of Your Organization

You won't find this information in the typical book about how to be an effective manager. To get maximum performance and loyalty out of any group of people, *it takes a combination of all the manipulative strategies you have been exposed to so far in these pages.* Strong management can rarely be accomplished by following naive rules in a scholarly textbook.

So, regardless of your ability to attract willing workers, you still need the vital knowledge of *how to exploit people* to make groups do exactly what you want them to do for you. Thus, the chapter you have just read about recruiting goes hand-in-hand with the one that follows. It's about *building a power structure.* In the pages that follow, you will discover tactics that keep your people operating at optimum capacity *for your benefit.* The rules hold true whether you're self-employed or working for someone. They also apply in almost every social situation you are apt to get involved in.

11

A Blueprint for Building Your Own Power Structure

To achieve victory, an army does not retreat back to its lines after winning a battle. *It occupies the captured ground so it can better control the future conduct of the war.* So it must be with you. After an organization is established, you have to *consolidate those gains.*

Even if you are in a situation that *doesn't* include the hiring of employees or agents, you can still be building a power structure for yourself. The point is, you should be busily at work making your environment favorable for *yourself,* and that can be accomplished whether you're a boss, an employee or whatever!

No matter *where* you are every day, and regardless of what you do to make a living, the potential around you is absolutely amazing! The trouble is, most people never *see* what the possibilities are. They simply go to work, put in their hours, go home, and repeat that mind-numbing process *without ever making the attempt to exploit their power-packed work surroundings!*

The fact is, a job—almost *any* job—can serve as a launching platform to bigger things. If *you* don't use it to get what you want, *someone else surely will.* This chapter shows how it can be done.

Getting Loyalty in Perspective

Before we get into the mechanics of how a power structure is established through normal business activities, a word about loyalty is important and timely. There is little doubt that many people fail to capitalize on their opportunities at work because they feel that somehow it would be detrimental to the company, to the people who sign the checks or to their fellow employees. That sentiment, in almost every instance, is misguided.

First of all, practically every business owner is interested in only one thing: *Making money*. They work on keeping good relations with employees only to the extent necessary to "hold the ship together." They are nice people only as long as profits stay healthy and reasonable harmony prevails among the help.

Some employees, as mentioned earlier, check into work like mindless robots. They are frequently indifferent to *anything* going on in their immediate environment as long as it doesn't jump up and bite them on the nose. They simply want to put in their time and collect a check on payday.

So what *is* loyalty? Very simply, it is the act of *not* doing anything to willfully *harm* the company you work for or its employees. But loyalty has nothing whatsoever to do with holding you back from using your job as a springboard to more power within the company—or better jobs with other firms!

To carry that reasoning one big step further, you would very likely become a *better* employee by practicing the tactics explained in this chapter. You would *certainly* be more valuable than the previously discussed clock-watchers who run home at the stroke of five o'clock!

So, don't worry about being labeled a troublemaker when you begin building a power structure in the firm you work for. Rather than be criticized, you'll probably be admired—*if* anyone even notices what you're up to!

Ross P's Program for Building Bridges to Personal Power

When Ross was a youngster, he constantly heard adults preach about the dangers of volunteering to undertake more than was absolutely necessary to get by. Fortunately, he never heeded that advice, and today he's executive vice-president of a petroleum refining company.

In the first job he ever held, as a clerk in the parts department of an automotive agency, Ross immediately began asking questions and absorbing knowledge. He was reprimanded more than once for leaving his station and visiting new and used car sales, the body shop, the accounting office and every other section of the business. Within 18 months, Ross had a view of the overall operation that he shared only with the owner of the agency and the general manager. By having an understanding of the interrelationships between various departments, he was in the unique position of being able to comprehend *everything he heard* from customers, clients and his superiors.

What was the advantage to Ross of being tuned-in to such a degree? Here's the answer: One small morsel of information that was utterly *meaningless* to most employees could be highly significant to the young clerk because he was able to *fit it into the big picture!* His knowledge of the *total workings* of the business enabled him to derive meaning from seemingly irrelevant details. On the other hand, *not* having that kind of big view of events is something like trying to tell what the subject of a jigsaw puzzle is by looking at one small piece!

But that's only the *first half* of a brilliant manipulative strategy. Knowing as much as he did, Ross *used* his knowledge to gain power in the organization. By observing what was taking place in *all* departments at once, it was frequently easy for Ross to *anticipate events anywhere from hours to days before they actually transpired.* His success rate was good enough to make a profound impression on both his fellow employees and bosses. He rapidly became known as an uncanny business observer, *despite his youth and inexperience.*

His skill became widely known and was eventually recognized; Ross was named general manager three years after joining the agency. Today, only ten years after starting his first job, he is a top executive in the oil industry.

The next section carries this strategy a step further.

"The Loyal Underground": How Audrey B's Allies Keep Her in Power

"Loyal Underground" sounds a bit sinister, but there is no better way to describe the network Audrey has established to maintain her grip on a big job with an equipment leasing company. It simply is not practical for her to personally travel around to various corporate departments as Ross P. does in the process of gathering valuable information. So Audrey has set up an underground organization that does the job for her.

First, Audrey carefully selects one person in each crucial department in the firm. Then she sets about the task of cultivating friendships with these men and women. As the friendships flourish, Audrey gradually creates a climate of mutual help; the other person tells the woman everything of significance that occurs in his or her department, in exchange for bits of gossip that Audrey discovers.

The phenomenon that takes place is most interesting. Audrey is able to arrive at important conclusions based on *the total* facts she is receiving from her various sources, but the individual sources get *nothing* of value from Audrey *because they are not getting the missing pieces of the puzzle!*

In building such a power structure, Audrey *never comes out and asks for information*. That is far too dangerous! Rather, she subtly approaches the subject as conversation inevitably gets into goings-on at the office. It's a delicate undertaking and must be handled gracefully. Before you even begin an attempt at trading information, be sure the people you select are loyal to you. If you have any doubts whatsoever about the integrity of your source, look further—or wait until a reliable individual becomes available.

One more caution: At all costs, avoid the trading of information that violates company security or in some way compromises the firm's reputation. The data you want from your underground is usually very general in nature *but takes on highly specific meaning when it is combined with the facts you collect from the other members of your network.*

Borrowing Connections to Reach Your Most Ambitious Goals

Your ability to collect information from various parts of a company through loyal allies, and your skill at making accurate predictions based on that data, will certainly put you a mile ahead of people who are content to spend their careers chained to the same desk. In a similar manner, *you can use your employer's suppliers and clients* to further enhance your position! Almost *every* company has a few hundred or more firms they do business with. To any skillful manipulator, this powerful lineup of companies can represent a fabulous opportunity for strengthening his power structure.

There are basically three ways in which this formidable outside force can benefit you:

1. *Again, information.* Both the suppliers and clients who do business with your employer are *loaded* with facts about what is going on in your firm. They also have a clear picture about events in the industry as a whole. So, by communicating with strategically located people in those organizations, you'll have a pipeline of crucial inside information that simply can't be beat.

2. *Feedback.* You can be sure that a tremendous volume of conversation goes back and forth between people in your company, and personnel in the firms that serve your employer. When you get yourself into a position of respect with those outside people, it's only a matter of time before favorable comments get back to your superiors. It works as well as the "grapevine" technique described in an earlier chapter.

3. *As a springboard to better jobs and more money.* This is the most obvious benefit of getting acquainted with your employer's suppliers and clients. When those people get to know you, and if they like what they see, the job offers will inevitably follow. The fact that there's a chance of souring a business relationship by stealing an employee does not often matter; if they want you, they'll find a way to get you!

Therefore, a vitally important part of your overall power structure lies in establishing connections with the people your firm deals with. It's a legitimate way of borrowing your boss's connections for your own advantage.

Now that we've covered the primary directions you can take in setting up your power structure, let's discuss a few of the strong methods you can use to consolidate your influence and control that private organization of yours.

Using the "Debt System" for Big Personal Gains

This is the way to build a "debt system": Whenever it is practical to do so, you would be wise to *refuse repayment of favors you do for the people you work with and socialize with.* At the same time, you should *quickly* repay favors done *for you by others!* One of the most effective ways to control the people in your power structure is to *have them owe you a favor.* While a cash debt all too often leads to strained relations between people, a moral debt usually does not. The principal advantage of having favors coming is the most obvious one: *You can cash in when you need it most.*

A less obvious reason is this: If you have friends in other departments who are funneling information to you, it helps tremendously if you hold I.O.U.'s on those individuals. That being the case, they are more likely to *remain* loyal to you. *Nobody wants to be accused of being ungrateful.* And the fact that you have granted a favor—but turned down repayment—will keep the information coming hot and heavy. So, you can keep your people on the hook by refusing returns of favors and trying as hard as you can to avoid becoming a debtor yourself! It keeps the would-be exploiters among your allies at bay.

Winning Important Objectives Through Obligations: How Alex G. Does it

Alex is a salesman for an industrial machine parts distributor. He *never* makes a sales call without handing both the receptionist and the purchasing agent of the prospective client company a small gift. He never gets involved in his pitch until he first asks about the other person's husband/wife and children, and Alex *remembers the names* of every person in all those families!

An anniversary, birthday, graduation or other major event in the life of a prospect or customer does not pass without Alex acknowledging that event by a card or phone call. An illness, even a minor one, brings some kind of consideration from this highly successful and thoughtful man. This concerted effort has put Alex at the lead in income and repeat business. Even the most difficult prospects find it hard to say "no" when he asks them for an order.

But this strategy does much, much more for Alex than just giving him a huge customer base and an income to match; it has given him a degree of control over his allies that is unsurpassed. For example, a large percentage of customers consult Alex before raising prices, changing policy, or doing anything else that might have an impact on the dealing between the two firms. Thus, *the salesman commands more loyalty and attention than his superiors do!* In effect, Alex has a say about proposed industry policy before it is made official.

With this kind of personal heft, Alex is able to control his own environment as surely as a puppeteer manipulates a marionette. To be sure, he doesn't *run* the companies that serve his employer, but he can *certainly* be considered a highly influential source.

As you have probably gathered, his strategy of showering people with recognition is a version of flattery. *It's an invaluable tool in keeping the people in your power structure cooperative, loyal and enthusiastic.*

Controlling Your People Through the Irritant-Planting Technique

A person who possesses the ability to solve problems will eventually end up in a position of leadership. The trouble is, problems that need solving don't always come along often enough to help the manipulator, so there has to be a way for you to *purposely create problems.* That way, you can be a master diplomat and troubleshooter *anytime you feel the need to strengthen your position and tighten your grip on the people in your power structure!*

The irritant-planting technique permits you to *manufacture* custom-made turmoil. In a company environment, this turmoil can be gossip about any number of topics. For example:

1. A rumor about cut-backs to be made in a certain department.
2. Talk of a takeover by another firm that would very likely result in staff changes.
3. Speculation about the possibility of responsibility shifts that might have an impact on key jobs.

There are scores of others. The point is, if you have established your network of allies (as described earlier in this chapter), you should be getting enough information to provide plenty of material for manufacturing turmoil. Here's how it might happen:

You receive word through your private pipeline that an operations manager is being considered for a vice-presidency. From another part of your network, you hear an unrelated piece of information to the effect that certain organizational changes are being contemplated for customer service.

These relatively innocent bits of scuttlebut can be *combined* by the manipulator (who is one of the only people in the firm who is aware of *both* rumors) and converted into a rather frightening parcel of bad news that definitely qualifies as an irritant. From the two unrelated rumors, *you create a story about Joe Smith getting his vice-presidency, then shaking up the customer service department.*

As the exploiter, you would *cautiously* plant this tale with a few of your local allies. Then, *just before* one of the events is to actually take place, you tell your people that you have inside information that Smith will probably *get* his vice-presidency, but has vowed to a few insiders that he wouldn't touch the customer service department. Presto! You were the first person in the company to provide very welcome news (that doesn't yet and may never exist!)

This strategy is simply an imaginative use of common information that floats around every organization. The difference is, instead of just sitting around and *listening* to predictions and rumors, you are making them work in your favor; you are, in the eyes of your allies, an individual who apparently has friends in very high places! Thus, their loyalty is assured.

Warning: Whatever you do, *don't* attempt to plant rumors with people who may not be loyal to you! This strategy should be utilized *only* with people who are unquestioned allies of yours. Remember, its purpose is to *strengthen their respect for you.*

Herb V's Method for Cementing Loyalty and Establishing Unquestioned Personal Influence

There is no doubt that many people will strongly object to the way Herb V. solidifies his position in the large manufacturing firm he works for. A middle-management executive, this man is probably headed for a top post in the company. He does maintain the same sort of underground described earlier, but he uses it strictly to gather gossip which is then "packaged" by him and passed on to higher-ups in the organization. Herb scores impressive points as the resident busybody.

The lower ranks in almost every large firm are teeming with opinions, stories, facts (both true and otherwise) and inevitable complaints. Any responsive management group wants to know the nature of this gab on a day-to-day basis. It helps the top people get a handle on what's going on, and it can sometimes help them steer clear of major morale problems. But *getting access* to the things the workers say is not always easy to do; a factory assembly-line employee, for example, will almost always be reluctant to confide in a vice-president. There is no faster way to be condemned by fellow workers!

That is precisely the missing link Herb provides. His personal network extends deeply into the rank and file. He has succeeded in maintaining the absolute trust of his sources because he takes the precaution of *packaging* the information he recieves before passing it on to his bosses. Here's how Herb packages the gossip he collects throughout each day:

> First, he'll take several bits of data, and combine them into a story. The story is always about a ficticious employee—but the *facts* remain accurate. In this way, Herb *protects his sources.* He is careful to eliminate any clue that might reveal specific people in his network.
>
> Secondly, Herb *tells* his sources that their information might be passed on to executives in the company. Of course, he reassures them that they will be protected at all costs. This honest approach has paid off.
>
> Finally, Herb has a system of rewards for his trusted contacts. They receive preferential treatment in ways that are not apparent to their fellow employees.

If there is *anybody* who comes close to being indispensible in this company, it is Herb V. If he leaves his job, the network collapses in a matter of hours. Thus, he is well cared for by the powers at the top, and his future seems assured.

The "Hands-Off" Control Phenomenon: A Must for Astute Manipulators

The kind of high-level political maneuvering we have talked about in this chapter requires discretion on the manipulator's part. As a case in point, Herb V. can't afford to be seen spending a lot of time chatting with his contacts in various company departments. He'd be suspected by just about *everyone* if he did. After initial rapport is established with key people, information is exchanged by telephone, by note or by personal meetings before or after business hours.

In the same way, you will find it advantageous to set up a hands-off system of command. This is actually a method that keeps you as far away as possible from the majority of your contacts. In effect, it's a multi-level organization that funnels information to a few higher sources. Ideally, you would be insulated by several layers of people by residing at the very top of this network.

Aside from discretion, the hands-off system offers you these benefits:

1. It encourages the creation of yet *another* information gathering organization, this one probably composed of higher-level individuals in a company. These are the people who act as intermediaries between you and your basic network. The additional "eyes and ears" definitely increase information input to you.
2. To repeat an important point, it *insulates* you and thus affords you protection. Here's an example: If one person in the network decides to announce to other workers that managment is getting the latest gossip, the problem stops at the next highest level. On the other hand, if you are collecting data *directly* from your contacts, you are much more exposed and vulnerable.

Whenever you see or hear of certain people being extremely adept in the highly competitive game of corporate politics, you can be *sure* they operate power structures similar to the ones we've discussed. It can take time to establish one, and it can be risky unless you're sure of the people you are dealing with. *But it is a fact of life in business. It's done every day, and done successfully by the most enterprising men and women in any organization large enough to support an underground network.*

One of the most efficient ways to recruit members of an underground network is through *assertive action.* The next chapter covers the essentials of this strategy.

12

Making Assertive Action Produce Amazing Windfalls

Possession is 90 percent of the law. You've undoubtedly heard that old saying more than once. It verifies the fact that *if you go through all the motions* of owning a particular object, almost everyone will believe it is yours, whether it actually is or not.

The saying, however, pertains to the possession of *physical objects.* It generally does not take into account relationships between people. What happens when a person automatically assumes a position of dominance over another without first bothering to be *declared* the dominant party?

This chapter describes what happens under those fascinating circumstances. And it tells you how to take that assertive position.

How Tommy A's Sports Tactics Made Him a Success in Life

Tommy's first invaluable lesson in *assertive action* came when he was eight years old. He discovered, quite accidently, that when he took it upon himself to act as both player *and* referee, he came out immeasurably further ahead. One day during an informal basketball game, Tommy thought he was fouled while driving to the basket for a shot. Rather than attempt to discuss the infraction with the opposing player, Tommy simply took the ball and walked to the sidelines to claim the out-of-bounds, as was customary in the case of a foul in those informal games.

Tommy wisely reasoned that to enter into negotiations with the offender and his teammates might have resulted in a lost argument, or worse, a fistfight. Not a soul in the game protested his quiet, yet determined action. The young man acted as if an official had blown the whistle and given him the verdict. Tommy quickly inbounded the ball to one of his players, and the game resumed. He realized *that to hesitate even one moment would have made him appear unsure of his position,* and without question would have drawn a challenge from the other side.

From that day on, in any sports event he participated in, Tommy was quick to take assertive action. He learned *never* to wait for someone else to arbitrate a dispute. It became obvious that *opponents usually let him have his way when he asserted himself in this way.*

In later years, when he entered the business world, Tom applied the same principles with enormous success. The following pages show you how this manipulative strategy works.

What's Mine Is Mine . . . What's Yours Is Ours

An important aspect of assertive action is *knowing how to accept things offered to you.* On the surface, it might appear that the correct action is simply to *take* what another person hands to you and be grateful for whatever it is. That's the reaction of most people, and it's exactly the kind of response sought by manipulators.

An example is this: You are a printer, and you are being considered (along with others) for a major project required by a large company. You are finally offered the job, and specifications, including prices, are presented to you in a written proposal. Faced with these circumstances, most recipients of such an offer would grab the assignment even if it was only marginally profitable. But a manipulative individual would tend to reason this way:

> *I've been selected for a definite reason, and it's most likely the quality I can deliver at a reasonable price. Also, I have good background in the particular areas this customer needs. That being the case, I feel comfortable in trying for as much money as I can get, because this client won't let me get away without a fight.*

So the printer takes bold action. He explains to the prospective client that they were wise in choosing him, but the proposed dollar amount would need to be increased. In addition, certain other conditions would have to be modified in favor of the printer.

This response is equal to *trying for the entire arm when only a hand is offered.* It takes guts sometimes because that nagging fear of losing business is always in back of the manipulator's mind. He may indeed lose an occasional client, *but assertive action definitely* opens the door to fabulous profit opportunities that would never make themselves available under ordinary circumstances.

In a nutshell, you should always be *strongly assertive* at the moment something is offered to you. Remember that the other party *rarely offers you the best deal initially.* So, by accepting quickly, you are giving away most of the gain that *should be coming to you!*

No matter how good a particular offer may seem—and regardless of how badly you may need whatever is being offered—*you must make it a rule to try for more.* The worst that could happen is that you'll end up negotiating, and perhaps a compromise will be reached. But in most instances, you'll come out *far ahead of those who meekly accept the first offer!*

Delores T. Tells How She Became a Business Owner Through the "Loose Entity" Phenomenon

You may occasionally discover a physical object that is owned by someone, but not claimed. When you encounter such a "loose entity," an assertive approach will almost always make the item yours if you wish to have it under those conditions.

People, however, are never really *owned* by anyone. Delores T., a minority stockholder in a thriving soft drink bottling company, recognized the similarity between unclaimed things and unclaimed people. She was so sure that she could take over men and women as easily as she could objects that she based an aggressive stock acquisition campaign on that strategy.

There were four minority stockholders in the bottling firm

besides Delores, plus one man who held a controlling interest. If the woman could somehow enlist the support of the other four, she could combine their shares with her own, and take over the firm. These four minority stockholders were, in the woman's view, *loose entities;* for all practical purposes, they were "ownerless." Separately, they would forever remain without power. But if Delores could "possess" them, they would become overnight factors in the running of the business—with her at the helm.

Delores never *asked* any of the four people for their backing (just as Tommy A. didn't bother asking the other basketball player if a foul was truly committed). She merely *took* their backing. She *assumed* there would be no objection to such a power play, and she also *assumed* that she was the leader of the minority rebellion! There were *no* challenges, *no* dissents. It seemed as though the four people *craved* the kind of powerful take-charge leadership Delores was providing. It also appeared that her silent assumptive action was overwhelmingly *preferred* by them, since they were spared the ordeal of discussing the takeover, which might have been embarrassing to the group. So it was happening without meetings, plots or schemes. Delores made the decisions and simply led her cohorts.

In a matter of weeks, the job was virtually complete. Delores was elected to the number one post in the firm. She had theorized that a loose entity phenomenon existed, and she was absolutely correct!

Using the Erosion Technique for Crumbling Gigantic Obstacles

Of course, it isn't always possible to possess things and people as quickly as Delores T. was able to do it. Even with the strongest kind of assertive action, major goals can be somewhat more difficult to attain. In these more stubborn cases, the erosion technique of assertion is the way to go.

Very simply, the erosion technique is the process of taking over people *in increments.* Instead of going for a grand sweep as Delores did, you take small pieces until the objective is accomplished. This method is extremely valuable where you suspect that the other person might react unfavorably to a strongly assertive move on your part.

The first step to making this strategy work is the creation of a plan. You set about defining and listing the small pieces you'll take over en route to total dominance. The following example illustrates how such a plan might work. It deals with a rather typical individual to make it as clear as possible for you:

> Your adversary is a middle-level executive and a contemporary of yours, since both of you are at the same rank in the company. You and the other person have certain well-defined responsibilities. The first thing you do is list the other person's chores, then plan an erosion strategy that will eventually give you control over the individual and his or her job.
>
> *The First Chore You Zero-In on:*
>
> *Your adversary is assigned the job of approving invoices before forwarding them to the accounts receivable office for payment.*
>
> *Your Strategy is as Follows:*
>
> a)You ask the person if you can begin checking the invoices as part of your routine. The pretext is that *you want to keep an informal record of expenses in your department,* which is innocent enough and sure to be granted without protest.
>
> b)After several weeks, you begin marking your initials, along with corrections, on invoices that are erroneous. You realize, of course, that the people in bookkeeping will notice who first detected the slip-ups (the fact that *you* now see them *before* your adversary is usually not considered!)
>
> c)A while later, you *tell* the head bookkeeper that effective tomorrow, *you will take the responsibility of screening invoices.*
>
> d)A few minutes after your talk with thc head book-

keeper, you *tell* your adversary that the head bookkeeper has approved a realignment of duties which puts the job of checking invoices in your lap, and that he no longer has to "waste his time" handling it.

The assertiveness and presumption of approval is *no less strong* than the way Delores does it, but it's a more gradual process, and therefore one that is far less likely to upset your adversary!

Here's a little different twist to the erosion technique and a method of assertion that works beautifully.

Albert's Law: Making Small Issues Turn into Major Triumphs

The chipping-away method of taking over is indeed an effective way to attain dominance while maintaining a reasonable degree of harmony with your adversary. Albert K., a furniture buyer for a large department store, uses a form of erosion to get his way. In order for him to compete favorably with other stores, Albert is faced with the necessity of creating a buying climate that gives him a clear advantage in his dealings with suppliers. In other words, he has to establish with every furniture factory a set of negotiating guidelines that give him the following edges, to name just a few:

1. That service from the factory will be immediate and unquestioned.
2. That discounts will at least equal, but more often exceed, those given to other stores.
3. That payment terms will be more lenient than competition receives.
4. That a certain number of *exclusive* sofa and table lines be developed for Albert's department.

These are tall orders, even for a large store. And Albert can't very well make demands of that magnitude when he *first meets* a new supplier. If he did, the factory would most likely take their wares elsewhere!

Albert's Law turned out to be the answer. Here it is:

By obtaining one minor concession per week, a relationship comes under your complete control by the end of one year.

The amazing thing about this phenomenon is that the weekly concession you gain can be so small as to seem insignificant. As a case in point, Albert might insist on 23-day delivery instead of the customary 26 days. The next week, he would demand from the same factory brass casters on all new sofas at no extra cost and so forth until the relationship is absolutely controlled by him!

Remember, Albert does not *ask* for these small advantages, he practically *assumes they are already granted!* He strongly asserts himself for those tiny extra details, and in time *the adversary becomes accustomed to giving up without a struggle.* By the end of a year (or less), Albert has *created a climate that is thoroughly in his favor,* and in doing so, the relationship remains as normal as it can be.

Let's take a closer look at the important area of preserving good will between yourself and your adversary. When you are making moves to take over and control people and events, maintaining harmony is a vital element.

The Art of Cementing Friendships While You Are Taking Over

It may appear to you that Delores T. and Albert K. set about their manipulative strategies with ruthlessness. It *is* true that virtually no obstacle can deter them, and people like them, from pursuing their objectives, but it's a misconception to think that these people-users go around grim and angry during every working day. The fact is, no matter how intensely you may practice assertive action—and the other exploitive tactics described in this book—*you still have to coexist in an environment with others.* And to get along with people, you simply can't be a villain or tyrant!

Therefore, you should work on developing a balance between a serious business-like demeanor on the one hand and a friendly outgoing side on the other. This balance does *not* include a tyrannical attitude in any way, shape or form. If people are antagonized by a manipulator, the strategies *will not work,* no matter *how* smoothly they are executed. Remember, you can take command while being pleasant as easily as you can by being serious. And *both* of those approaches are vastly superior to wearing a scowl.

How the Taking of Space Can Lead to the Seizing of Influence

The gaining of territory is the growth of power. When applied to everyday events in the lives of average men and women, this is what that means:

> *The more space you can claim as your own in a business or social environment, the more power and influence you'll obtain.*

"Space" might be offices, special responsibilities, jurisdiction over other employees and possibly even supervisory authority over machines and other facilities. Although you may not *own* these people or things in the strict sense of the word, *you still hold most of the aces when you command them!*

There are countless "loose entities" in the typical business or social setting. Plenty of space is unclaimed, and many people wander around aimlessly, as we have discussed before. As a seeker of power, *you can take control of this territory by simply using assertive action.*

You may wonder how such gains can be retained if your control is challenged. The answer to that question lies in the following extremely smart tactic.

How Ellis G. Uses the Formidable "Burden of Proof" Tactic to His Enormous Advantage

Ellis manages a small department in the headquarters operation of a national construction company. The competition among middle management people is fierce; it isn't at all surprising that success in the firm depends on surviving this tough in-fighting. With a relatively minor role in the overall operation, Ellis' department appeared to be out of the running as far as influence was concerned, and it followed that his personal future was equally doubtful.

Despite these major obstacles, Ellis ended up as the most important manager among his peers within two years of starting with the organization! The key to this extraordinary achievement was *assertive action.* The young manager constantly had his eyes open, looking for *loose entities* around the company.

His first acquisition was a secretary whose boss was on an extended foreign business trip. Ellis discovered that she was spending much of her time doing "busy work" during the absence of her superior. Ellis wasted no time in seeing to it that she was transferred to his group.

Next, he picked up a small office that had recently been converted from a storeroom but remained vacant. Ellis had his people occupy the room the same day he discovered it, *then* sent a memo to his boss which matter-of-factly described his action!

This expansion continued gradually until Ellis controlled considerable "real estate" on the second floor of the building, and his staff was swollen to nearly twice its prescribed size. But, the genius of his strategy is in his ability to *retain* conquered property. When Ellis is challenged by other managers (which happens about half the time), *he quickly places the burden of proof on the challenger.* His adversary must provide convincing evidence that Ellis was not entitled to what he had taken!

A *weak* response from Ellis would result if he attempted to justify his acquisition. This is equal to going on the defensive and is the most feeble possible reaction. As far as the manager is concerned, the person or thing is *his.* He *believes* that possession is 90 percent of the law!

Therefore, the *challenger* is the one who is attempting to encroach on claimed territory and is thus the one who must prove that Ellis acted without proper authority. The proof, if any, usually fails to change anything, and Ellis becomes stronger and stronger. The combination of assertive action and burden of proof is propelling him to the top quickly.

A plan follows that is designed to speed up your progress in becoming a skilled collector of territory.

A Never-Fail Five-Step Program for Becoming an Owner of People and Things

These guidelines provide the step-by-step methods you need to master assertive action:

1. *Review the Way You React When the Opportunity to Acquire a Loose Entity Presents Itself.* Most people cave in when they have a chance to be assumptive. For some reason, they become timid and turn their backs on things or people that reach out for a new "owner."

   Next time an opportunity comes along, stop a moment and *look into yourself.* If you feel yourself shying away from strong assertive action, *remember that just a few more moments of strength will bring you personal gains.*

2. *As Soon as You Overcome the Tendency to Back Off, Try Your New Assertive Strength on a Small Objective.* Experiment with acquiring an *object* of some sort before you take on another person. Be patient and wait for a loose entity to come along. It might happen at your place of work, or it may be something in your personal life.

   The main thing is, *you'll be ready* when it comes along, and the ability to move quickly and decisively is all-important. Fast action in assuming control knocks adversaries off balance, and you take possession before they can protest.

3. *When You Feel Ready to Assume Control Over a Person, Start by Trying Assertive Action on Someone You Just Met and Will See Often in the Future.* A *new* acquaintance doesn't know what to expect from you, and will react more spontaneously than an old friend or associate who is probably accustomed to a less aggressive approach from you. An individual you know from the past might not buy your new power.

In short-term relationships, it sometimes doesn't pay to make a takeover attempt since no benefits are likely to come your way. But, if you'll be socializing with or working closely with the individual, go ahead and get control. Being close also gives you the opportunity to monitor your grip on the relationship. This is important, since it is beneficial to be able to *sustain* a commanding position.

4. *At Every Chance You Get, Practice Seeing People and Things as Yours.* Go back to the earlier chapter in this book about *visualizing.* You can train yourself to *be* an owner if you simply *see yourself* as an owner!

   Whenever it's convenient, create situations in your mind where you run across loose entities (either people or things) and assert control over them. Your proficiency will increase dramatically.

5. *Get in the Habit of Assuming Dominance Over All Loose Entities, Important or Not.* Even if you know that a particular material acquisition will not be useful to you, *claim it anyway.* This sharpens your assumptive power and cultivates your ability to *see* opportunities.

An essential part of taking command is your ability to win the relatively small encounters you come across nearly every day of your life. The next chapter brings you those valuable tactics.

13

Winning Strategies You Can Use Every Day of Your Life

Some of the major manipulative strategies discussed so far in this book are effective over extended periods of time; they are designed to *gradually* move you into positions of dominance. Depending upon the actual circumstances, it can take several days to a few months for you to gain your objectives. But what about the *daily* skirmishes all of us experience? Should these numerous encounters be ignored for the sake of victory in only the long range goals? No! It is extremely important for you to *win all the small confrontations* you undergo during each and every day.

This kind of mastery over people and events will significantly enrich and improve the quality of your life. The *smallest, briefest transactions you enter into will be controlled by you.* You'll never again have that unpleasant feeling of being taken advantage of.

This chapter is devoted to describing the most effective of these day-by-day manipulative tactics.

Gil R's Rule for Becoming Valuable in the Blink of an Eye

Gil is a gifted commercial artist. His illustrations are highly valued by advertising agencies, plus he claims a strong following, which he cultivated on a free-lance basis. From the time he first started getting worthwhile prices for his work, Gil was beset by friends and relatives who wanted special drawings from him.

These requests were invariably for "little sketches—nothing elaborate." These words inferred that Gil was not expected to spend much time on the work and would not charge for his trouble, since it was only expected to take a "moment."

Countless favors like the one described above occupied over

one hour of every working day and frequently much more. In terms of his normal rates, that represented $150 to $250 in lost income to Gil every 10 days. Such a loss eventually forced the artist to take a long, hard look at his way of handling the growing number of non-paying clients that besieged him.

Gil's solution was simply *to quote his hourly rate every time such a request came up*, and it didn't matter *who was asking*. Even close friends, aunts and uncles were informed that his time demanded hard cash!

This change in the illustrator's method of operation made an immediate difference in Gil's professional life. It freed him for more important assignments and dramatically improved billings. But the impact of his new attitude reached *non-business* aspects of the artist's life as well. He now *refused* to give away *any* of his time, even so-called leisure time!

This new attitude really turned things around for the young man. *By putting a specific dollar value on every hour of his daily life, Gil made a valuable property of himself.* Although a few people were slightly shocked by his new position, most people started to look up to him as they never had before. But, *most* important, *everyone* now realized that Gil was no soft touch.

One of the greatest services you can do for yourself *right now* is to *set a price on your time and stick to it*. Don't give away another moment! Protecting yourself from being pushed around begins with placing definite values on your precious minutes. Let's take this protective strategy to the next level in order to see how you can come out ahead when you are in the role of a consumer.

Turning Consumer-Consciousness into Immediate Personal Benefits

Many retail stores and service companies take unmerciful advantage of their customers. This is so prevalent that it is a definite factor in reducing the quality of daily life. Therefore, if you utilize a different approach in your dealings with merchants, your life should take an immediate turn for the better.

For just a moment, look at this situation through the eyes of an exploitive business owner. The enterprise is well established, and customer traffic has increased tremendously in a period of several years. It's no longer necessary for the boss to follow-up closely on every transaction. Things now seem to happen without any real effort—and without the top person's immediate involvement.

In circumstances like these, the fate of the consumer is in the hands of store employees who are often not qualified to render customer satisfaction or who simply *do not care enough to try.* The results, all too often, are flagrant abuses of shoppers.

But are shoppers defenseless? Absolutely not. The consumer has more heft today than in past years. Consumer protection organizations and local government fraud divisions have helped to change things, so you now have a *voice* when someone tries to short-change you. Here's how to *use* that voice:

1. *Demand* courtesy and attention. *You are entitled to it!* Don't *ever* take it for granted that you should shop on a self-service basis.
2. Insist on as much information as you need to make a sound buying decision. Again, you should *not* accept neglect from lazy or indifferent employees!
3. When you encounter defects, or poor quality, or overpricing, *don't just "write it off" and forget it,* as so many shoppers do. Go back to the store and raise as much fuss as you have to in order to get satisfaction!
4. *Go directly to the boss* when problems arise. Trying to get service from an employee who has no authority—and no real concern—is futile. Do *not* agree to negotiate with anybody less than the owner or someone in a very high position. That is *your privilege* as a customer!

Control over this seemingly small part of your life will help establish strength patterns in your makeup. These relatively minor victories will reenforce the habit of winning the bigger contests.

The increasing "bigness" of today's business and institutions contributes to our loss of identity. Many of us have let ourselves become mere numbers. The following is a description of how this works and how you can avoid it.

The "Cattle Car" Syndrome

People in power eventually lose their concern for the average person because most individuals don't seem to care one way or the other *how* they are treated. As long as most men and women *accept* being prodded along in a faceless crowd, that's exactly how they'll be handled. For example, a store might cut expenses by eliminating one checkout register; they feel confident about the decision because customers *go along* with the longer lines and delays. A major entertainment attraction's owners think nothing of packing several hundred customers into a tiny waiting area and making them stand around for up to two hours before they can enter the grounds. Their admission money, of course, is taken *before* the wait!

These are classic examples of the "cattle car" syndrome. It's an appropriate name because that's precisely how cows are herded about. The people who submit to procedures like these are being used. But worse than that, *they are being conditioned to accept roles of subservience in the future.* You might think there is no way to combat treatment like this. That's exactly what the proprietors of these places *want* you to think! There *are* ways to escape the cattle car. Here's how one very strong woman does it.

Bernadine L's Three Tools for Cutting Tons of Red Tape and Formality

Bernadine first learned not to accept subservience when she was 18 years old. Up to that point in her life, she quietly went along with almost any kind of abuse others handed out. She simply went along with the crowd. But one day, the young woman bought an expensive dress for a school social event. The difficulty began when it was time to pay for the clothing.

Bernadine encountered such rudeness and indifference from the store clerks that she became enraged. The department manager was summoned, and after a brief but heated discussion between the teenager and the store employee, Bernadine was suddenly treated like visiting royalty! The episode convinced her that there would *never be another incident in her life when people would be permitted to ignore her.* No matter what it took to command respect and attention, Bernadine would do it.

A plan eventually evolved that accomplished exactly what she was after. It consists of three basic manipulative strategies, and she can draw on the one that seems to fit her immediate needs best. Here they are:

1. *Assertive Action*

   Bernadine *takes* when the taking is good. She doesn't wait for some authority figure to come around and *tell* her what she can or cannot do. Here's one case in point:

   Bernadine pulled her car into a public parking garage near the building where she had a business appointment. She immediately saw that the attendants were in no rush to serve her—and she had only five minutes to spare if she was to be on time. Although the sign in front of her clearly said "WAIT HERE," *she pulled into the first available space and began walking to the street.*

   Did *that* get action! An attendant hurried after her and gave her a claim ticket. Without this assumptive move, Bernadine might have waited *ten minutes!* (The open parking spot, incidentally, represented a loose entity).

2. *Fear*

   The new consumer consciousness described earlier in this chapter is used to tremendous advantage by Bernadine. She has perfected a fear tactic based on it and uses this strategy to get the best possible treatment stores can give. She does it this way:

   As soon as she sees there will be unusual delays, or the moment it becomes apparent that the attitudes of store help are marked by indifference, Bernadine goes straight to the person obviously in charge of the department, then politely and quietly announces that *she will not tolerate shabby service.*

Astute managers *know* about "people like this woman," and rather than take a chance on a commotion in clear view of other shoppers (a nightmare for any store executive), they *make sure* she gets waited on quickly!

This may seem like an extreme measure to take, but it virtually assures red carpet service for the manipulator!

3. *Flattery/Promises*

Bernadine realizes that many overworked employees will *not* respond to assertiveness or fear. In fact, quite a few of these people are recognition starved and would thus be susceptible to flattery and compliments. When she senses this, Bernadine does the following:

She corners a store employee and *insists* that he or she wait on her because of the clerk's "apparent competence." The person usually drops everything else and concentrates on helping Bernadine. The woman tells the clerk that she'll make sure store management finds out about the excellent service she's receiving. Needless to say, the average unappreciated worker becomes putty in her hands!

Here's a gentleman who has another way of making sure he's handled with kid gloves.

Mario S. Tells How Declaring a Code of Principles Puts Him on the Inside Track

Mario finds that it isn't always necessary to resort to manipulative tactics to command respect and attention in his daily encounters. In rare instances, he is automatically treated well just by entering an establishment. And in other instances, it simply takes *a declaration of principles from him.* This declaration consists of letting the people you are dealing with know *what you demand* in the way of service and respect. This strategy is based on the premise that most individuals in power really don't know that there *are* a small number of consumers who *do care* about how they are treated.

Mario's tendency is to give people the benefit of the doubt; he'd rather not use fear, threats or assertiveness where he can avoid it. So he decided to *tell* adversaries what he expects of them *before* the relationship gets started. Here's what his *Code of Principles* is and how he delivers it:

> First, as soon as the man enters an establishment, he locates someone in a position of authority. He tells that person he wants to make a purchase and how he's accustomed to being waited on in other places around town.
>
> Depending on the circumstances, Mario might declare that he's been subjected to poor service in the past . . . that he's a valued customer . . . or any number of other reaons why the place and its people had better serve him well.

Invariably, he is waited on by a higher-up who bends over backward to help him. An example of the impact Mario's tactics have made is this: In the better restaurants in town, he is now greeted by the owner or manager on a first-name basis, and he is immediately led to the best table in the house! Mario simply told those people that he *expected* such treatment.

The "Change-of-Pace" Tactic for Instant Results

Some of your simple day-to-day encounters may involve people you have occasion to deal with often. They are not just one-time meetings. In these established relationships, patterns have most likely been set that make both you and the other person rather predictable to each other. You and your adversary know what to expect and act accordingly. Chances are, the one who was successful in seizing dominance initially (when you first met) is still the one in control.

The best way to break a losing pattern like this is through the "change-of-pace." If you train yourself to *act* just a little, you can keep your adversary off balance by *being a different person whenever you choose!* You'll be called moody, temperamental, unpredictable and worse. But the people who have taken you for granted in the past *will now begin handling you with extreme care!* The change-of-pace will shatter the control others may have over you.

You shouldn't carry this strategy to extremes, because it *can* becomes exceedingly confusing to others. But it's most effective when done *just often enough to make you difficult to predict.*

Let's look at a cosmetologist who is a master at the change-of-pace.

Bea M's Way of Commanding Special Attention in Most Daily Contacts

Nobody, but *nobody,* ever takes Bea for granted. In the beauty shop she runs, the customers have tremendous respect for her and return time after time. Her staff is under the woman's firm control every minute of every working day. She is unquestionably the absolute master of her environment.

Being "nice" did not accomplish this enviable situation for Bea. She realized years ago that merely being agreeable didn't always work that well, because there were always people who attempted to take advantage of easygoing individuals. Besides that, Bea sensed that people gradually became bored by those with perfectly even dispositions, so she decided to be spontaneous. Bea wanted to see how people would react to her *if she displayed how she felt.* At least, it might stir up the environment in her shop, which had lately become noticeably stale.

At first, Bea found herself holding back. She was subconsciously reluctant to let her moods break through to the surface where others could *see* them. But, as time went on, it became easier and more natural for her to demonstrate her feelings. Happiness bubbled up as Bea felt it, anger flared at precisely the instant she experienced it and thoughtful moods reflected as an uncharacteristic quietness from the cosmetologist. *Customers, employees and everyone else watched the woman with renewed fascination and respect!* She changed from a rather bland shop owner to a magnetic personality.

Bea was overwhelmed by the reaction and quickly decided to transform the phenomenon into a science. Now, instead of *waiting* for mood changes, *Bea can become just about anything she wants to be in an instant!* She can select the best approach for the moment at hand and keep people on their toes. Bea is considered one of the most colorful and commanding personalities in her community!

Win Daily Encounters by Protecting Your "Weakness Buttons"

Early in this book, we spoke of programming that virtually every human being is subjected to from childhood. Like computers, we are set up to react in certain ways to things that happen to us in life. Unfortunately, the ways we learn to react do not necessarily reflect the beliefs we really feel.

As you know, bad programming like this can make most people terribly weak. They can never truly assert themselves, or act of their own free will. Therefore, *success in daily encounters* depends on the rooting out of this bad programming.

The time to start changing *is the very next time somebody tries to "push your button" in order to get one of those built-in responses from you!* Here are two very typical examples of how your button might be pushed:

1. If you're a woman, you hear "Go wash the dishes, so we can go out later."
   Very often the response to this request is, "*Of course*, it's my job to do the dishes. My mother does them, my sister does them and most of my friends do them."

2. If you're a man, you hear, "The faucet is leaking, please take care of it".
   The male *accepts* this responsibility without question. After all, his father and brothers do it, and it's *a man's job*.

So, it doesn't take much imagination to see how you can be controlled through your bad programming if you're an employee. It won't take a manipulative boss or fellow worker long to figure out where your buttons are. What you have to do beginning *now,* is look into yourself more carefully than ever before to find out *what makes you jump.* Are you reacting the way *you* want to react, or are you letting your life be run according to somebody elses standards?

The job of protecting yourself against other manipulators deserves much more than just a few words. The concluding chapter of this book is devoted to a number of very successful strategies that will *keep you beyond the reach of exploiters.*

14

Making Yourself Manipulation-Proof

To make the most of life, you have to participate in your daily existence to the total extent of your being. This will bring you valuable new friendships, a multitude of financial opportunities, and all the other benefits and joys that come along during the average lifetime. There is, however, this potential flaw in such an open approach to life:

> By opening yourself up to every possible opportunity—and by seeking out new people-relationships—you will inevitably *become more of a target to people-users who want to get you entangled in their webs.* This occurs because you are far more visible than you would be if you hid from society.

This holds true even if you are engaged in manipulative strategies of your own! It's something like the hunter being hunted.

So, it is *extremely* important for you to keep your guard up despite the fact that you may be on the offensive. Letting somebody get control of you can seriously slow down your progress toward the goals you have set for yourself, *whatever* those goals happen to be.

The tactics covered in this chapter do *not* suggest burying your head in the sand to escape the influence of exploiters. Instead, they are designed to let you *remain* in the mainstream of life, where you *should* be.

One of the Most Power-Packed Words in the English Language

An eminently successful businessman once said, "By answering 'no' to almost every request made of me, I have advanced far faster than I would have under normal circumstances. Through this simple device, I've managed to steer clear of nonproductive obligations, and I have nicely avoided being a money lender in situations where I knew I wouldn't be paid back. In addition, the 'no' response has given me something of a colorful reputation; I'm considered tough by my associates, and that hasn't hurt my business progress a bit."

The fact is, many people have extreme difficulty saying "no". This is especially true if a request comes up suddenly and you are faced with making an on-the-spot decision. The rule should be, *unless you have had plenty of time to carefully arrive at a yes answer, your response must always be a flat, clear-cut "no"!* In other words, whenever you have even the *tiniest shred of doubt,* your answer is "no."

The basic principles behind this tactic are as follows:

1. After you respond negatively, you can always soften your stand and change to a "yes." In fact, your adversary will have much more appreciation for your change-of-mind than if you had answered "yes" when the request was first made.
2. After you answer "yes" initially, it's exceedingly difficult to switch to a "no" later. It makes you look weak and indecisive. Therefore, take the hard line from the very beginning to appear as strong as possible.
3. Most important, as you gain a reputation that characterizes you as "a tough nut to crack," the people around you will make requests *only* when they are sure you'll go along. And when they *do* ask for your time or cooperation, they'll make sure there's something in it for you, which is a giant stride toward being manipulation-proof.

While it is an amazingly potent anti-exploitation weapon, the word "no" can seem rather crude in some instances. This is how one woman makes it a little easier on those who try to use her.

How Thelma K. Makes "No" Sound Like "Yes"

As a middle-level executive for a small town local TV station, Thelma is besieged with requests for favors. Almost all of them come from people who want to use her as a connection to break into the broadcast industry at one level or another. As you would imagine, the word "no" is used frequently by the woman. But, because she is deeply concerned with preserving good relations in the small community, Thelma delivers the word in gift wrapping.

A flat "no" would shock and insult many people. So Thelma came up with a negative response that builds up the ego of her adversary. Those who are turned down by her walk away *feeling good about themselves—not* deflated and rejected.

In one case, an acquaintance asked the TV executive if there was any chance of getting an audition for a newscaster role. Instead of a discouraging refusal, Thelma answered this way:

> "You probably have the basic requirements to make it as a newscaster, but I'd do you a serious injustice by helping you start with this station. The way to approach it is to get formal training. With that, you'd be in a position to rise to the top of the field. I promise my total support as soon as you get professional preparation."

Thelma knows full well that practically *nobody* is willing to make a commitment to that extent. Formal training requires money, time and dedication. Therefore, she promises her unqualified support *if* difficult preconditions are met by the other individual. *The preconditions always pertain to the ultimate improvement of the person who is making the request of Thelma.* Thus, the individual is left with the feeling that Thelma is vitally concerned with their well-being. The negative, put this way, has to be the most encouraging "no" the person has ever heard!

This system of building up your adversary can be used in virtually any situations where you find yourself being asked for time or other favors. Thelma also has occasion to use the next tactic in remaining free of people who want to use her.

Preemptive Declarations Can Change Your Life

By being on the alert for those seeking favors, Thelma is able to use the "preemptive declaration" for keeping people-users at safe distances. It's one more way besides "no" to remain free.

The preemptive declaration is simply a statement *designed to prevent another person from asking for your time or efforts.* In military terms, it's a "first strike" that stops the adversary before he can get his attack underway. This is the way it works:

As soon as you sense a request coming, you quickly cut the other person short (*before* he or she gets to the expected point), and you deliver a strong reason or two why the anticipated request can't be granted. For example:

> Let's say you're having a friendly cup of coffee with an acquaintance who you believe wants your talents or time for his own benefit. As the conversation progresses, you feel him moving toward the question itself. *At this point, you seize control of the conversation (as subtly and smoothly as you can) and begin explaining about how busy you are.*

You have to work on making your preemptive declaration look spontaneous. It *shouldn't* appear to be a reaction to the other person's line of conversation.

In nine out of ten cases, this tactic will head your adversary off at the pass, and you'll be spared the necessity of saying "no." In fact, *anytime* you are able to predict what is on another person's mind, you can use this strategy to control the direction of the relationship.

The next anti-exploitation tactic we'll discuss is intended to combat *fear.*

How Trudy O. Blows Holes in Bluff

A secretary for nine years, Trudy's entire career was impaired by fear. She worried about job security, about what others thought of her, about getting on the wrong side of her superiors and about *everything* that represented even the most vague threat to her. This attitude made Trudy a prime target for manipulators who recognized and understood the use of threats. As a result she was *constantly* being used.

The secretary actually came upon the solution to her problem accidentally. One Thursday afternoon, Trudy's boss asked her to work over the coming weekend. As it happened, she had plans to visit friends in a nearby city and couldn't possibly comply with the request. She explained her plans to the executive, but knowing her vulnerability to fear, he told her to make different arrangements, or else her refusal to work would be considered when raise time came around.

Instead of reacting in panic and backing down as she usually did, Trudy politely but firmly let her boss know that she fully intended to *go through* with her weekend away and that failure to obtain the scheduled raise would cause her to report the man's unreasonable demand and to resign from the company.

This time, *her boss* backed off! The following month, Trudy got her pay raise. And she also received this bonus. From the moment she stood up to that threat, her status increased dramatically. Trudy discovered the fact that *most threats are nothing but hot air.* They were being created *by the very fear she was displaying to people,* and the moment she stopped being frightened by her own shadow, the threats vanished!

There follows a remarkably strong remedy for being taken in by baseless promises.

Edwin C. Plays it Smart and Gets it in Writing

Most people really do have blind faith in others. The truth is, a little suspicion and cynicism would serve them far better. An example is Edwin C. No matter how smoothly his business relationships progress—and regardless of how personally involved he gets with the other individual—*he always asks for a signed agreement that summarizes what he will give and receive in a particular transaction.*

Even the *smallest* deals are formalized. In some instances, he scrawls a few lines on an envelope or business card, and both he and his adversary initial it. This procedure might seem strange to you, but Edwin claims that it *all but eliminates exaggeration from the other party during negotiations and strongly reinforces the likelihood that the deal will ultimately be fulfilled.*

The most striking part of Edwin's strategy is the way he introduces his impromptu contract:

1. First, he produces a piece of whatever paper is readily available, even if it's a napkin. This makes it appear as if his desire to list the points is purely spur-of-the-moment.
2. Edwin proceeds to scribble down the essential agreement, all the while asking his adversary for verification. At this point, it appears to the other person that the writing is simply a kind of note-taking; he or she doesn't *dream* that a signature will soon be requested!
3. This step is crucial and it is handled delicately by Edwin. He tells the other person that he trusts him beyond question, and that although a handshake will be sufficient to seal the deal, he feels it's good business for both of them to initial or sign the casual document in order to avoid any chance of misunderstanding.

When Edwin puts it that way, scarcely anybody he deals with declines to sign the paper. And if they *did* balk at this stage, he would have good reason to suspect that person's intentions to follow through.

So far, this man hasn't been taken advantage of! Even though his collection of informal contracts probably wouldn't stand up in a court of law, they *are* a potent deterrent to cheating!

Let's turn to an effective weapon against flattery.

Motive-Hunting: Alicia's Sure-Shot Way to Find Out if She's Being Buttered-Up

As mentioned earlier in this chapter, a little cynicism can serve you well, *especially* when flattery comes your way! Alicia is purchasing director for a medical supply company. In that position, she has learned to separate manipulative compliments from sincere praise. To make this sometimes difficult distinction, she uses the "motive-hunting" technique.

One excellent way to uncover *any* ulterior motive is simply to *wait*. Here's a case in point:

> The purchasing director was recently invited to lunch by an X-ray equipment salesman from whom she regularly purchased supplies. Within ten minutes of the time they sat down at the table, Alicia was listening to the man talk about how remarkable it was that she, a wife and mother, could handle such responsibility in a demanding career.

While he was going on and on about her successful struggle in a man's world, Alicia was wondering whether she was hearing a line, or a genuine compliment. If it *was* a line, she knew that he would soon attempt to introduce a new product (since she was *already* buying his items, the ulterior motive could *only be something new* that his company wanted to introduce). But, if it was sincere, they would finish lunch and go their separate ways without a sales pitch. Alicia listened to the man attentively and thanked him for his compliments. Then, sure enough, out came the brochure showing a few pieces of new equipment! The woman was ready, thanks to her silent cynicism.

Many people would be swept off their feet by such a carefully contrived package of softsoap. And by the time a people-user was ready to spring the trap, the victim would be ripe for the close. Therefore, motive-hunting is merely the act of *waiting for the punchline.* When the compliments start to flow, you listen with detached interest, then sit back and *see what follows!* The key is this:

While you are doing your best to look as if the praise is having an effect, *you are actually letting it bounce off that armor plate you use for just such a situation.*

Then, if your waiting game does *not* produce an ulterior motive, you can feel perfectly safe in dropping the armor and enjoying the apparently real flattery.

Here's one more way to make *waiting* work wonders for you.

Buying Time Can Keep You Free as a Bird

Almost any time you are faced with warding off the steamroller effect of assertive action from another manipulator, procrastination can be your best friend. Arguing will *not* prevent your adversary from grabbing loose entities, and attempting to reason with that person will often fail. When you feel yourself being rushed into a decision, assertive action is almost certainly being used to control you. The great majority of people succumb to pressure like this, and they wind up being owned by those who really understand the workings of assertiveness.

People who *rebel* against assertiveness only succeed in giving up control of their own lives. Getting upset and turning your back is just one more way of burying your head in the sand. That definitely isn't the answer.

But procrastination *is* the experienced exploiter's way to do battle with a fellow manipulator. Imagine a situation where you are being shoved into a decision. Rather than lose your temper at the pressure, you respond like this:

> It's a great idea, and I really think it's for me. But I want to consider every possible angle before we finalize. Between now and the next time we meet, I'm going to consider every last detail to be sure we don't miss anything.

No manipulator can resist that. He or she *has to* come back for the "kill." But when your next meeting *does* take place, *you* are ready with a counter proposal that GIVES *YOU* THE ADVANTAGE!

If your offer is refused, at the *very least* you have remained free of the person's grip. Remember, *time takes the edge off an attack.* Therefore, if you can manage to put off manipulators, you'll find that *your strength in the relationship tends to grow faster and becomes more powerful than the other person's.*

Assaults on your confidence can easily be repulsed. Let's take a look at how it's done.

Creating Instant Immunity to Downgrading

There are only two reasons on earth why anyone would use downgrading on you:

1. To get your services at a reduced rate—at terms favorable to that person. If this is the case, the downgrading usually has no basis in truth, and is being *invented by your adversary strictly for the purpose of using you.*

2. People who lack self-confidence—or who don't like themselves—might downgrade you. They belittle others at any opportunity just to make themselves feel better for some perverse reason. They are not people-users in any sense, and there is no strategic purpose to what they do.

In either case, you can see that downgrading *has no real substance.* But when it is directed at us, we *forget* that fact and take it personally. And when it's taken to heart, it can make people sell themselves short!

So, the objective is to *avoid becoming emotional* when you hear yourself being torn down. By remaining cool and collected, you are striking the hardest blow possible at your adversary. A passive counter attack of this kind packs more punch than *anything else* you could do under these circumstances! In fact, a *smile* on your face adds to the devastation you direct back at your adversary.

The most interesting thing about such an unemotional, passive defense to downgrading is that as soon as your adversary discovers that the attack is being repelled like a snowball off armor plate, *he or she suddenly becomes extremely vulnerable to you!* After the smoke clears, you can often move in and take over with ease!

An Infinitely More Powerful You in One Week or Less

Is there any mystery surrounding the tactics that have been described for you in this book? You have to agree there is not. Did it prescribe anything you would be unable to do in the process of controlling people and events? You have to agree it did *not.* All it takes is *practice,* plus the fascinating art of *watching people* and *evaluating them* in the privacy of your own mind.

You don't have to absorb the fine points of each section before you can begin to change into a powerful leader. You have, *right now,* enough knowledge to make dramatic strides toward a position of eminence in your job, at home and in your social environment.

The moment you read the final word in this volume, you'll be ready to start turning things around. The first person you encounter will offer you an experience such as you've never had before. Here's why:

1. For the first time in your life, you'll feel *real strength* when you meet a new acquaintance.
2. You now have the ability to *see into* that person. This will make your relationship with the individual far more satisfactory and manageable than people-associations have ever been for you in the past.
3. No matter *what* sort of events occur in that new relationship, you'll understand *precisely* what you have to do *to seize and maintain control.* The situation will *not* get away from you *unless you want it to!*

Therefore, the next week in your life promises to be *astonishingly different.* And, as you gain experience in using manipulative tactics, you'll get increasingly more adept at handling people.

But, whatever you do, try to *remain* a student of people! Referring to the chapters in this book periodically will reinforce your ability to a degree that will absolutely amaze you!

Index

A

B

C

R

S